WORKING WINDOWS

A GUIDE TO THE REPAIR AND RESTORATION OF WOOD WINDOWS

TERENCE MEANY

The Lyons Press

Printed in the United States of America

Designed by Benchmark Productions, Inc.

10 9 8 7 6 5 4 3 2 1

Library of Congress Cataloging-in-Publication Data.

Meany, Terence. 1953–
    Working windows: a guide to the repair and restoration of wood windows / Terence Meany.
        p. cm.
    Includes bibliographical references.
    ISBN 1–55821–707-X
    1. Wooden windows—Maintenance and repair. I. Title.
TH2275.M43   1998
690'.1823—dc21   98–10244
                                                            CIP

Grateful acknowledgment is made to the following trademarked products mentioned in this book: WonderBar, Peel Away, DAP, Bondo, LiquidWood, WoodEpox, and 3M V-Seal Door Weatherstrip.

CONTENTS

FOREWORD

As a home repair columnist with Universal Press Syndicate and the "How-To" Expert Editor for Amazon.com, the online bookstore, I run across, investigate, and review a *lot* of home repair books these days.

One of my consistent disappointments has been the sketchy, impractical information about the repair and maintenance of wood windows. Many books have a tiny bit of information, most of which involves photographs of drawings of clean, neat, mostly brand-new windows. Living in San Francisco and functioning as an active handyman since 1985, my experience of wood windows is a bit different.

Peeling paint, rotten lower rails, parting strips gunked up with layers of paint and nailed in place, upper sash glued in place by repetitive painting—these are more what I have seen. I know for a fact that many people do not realize that the upper sash in a double-hung wood window is meant to be cleaned easily from the interior, if working properly, and will last virtually forever if properly maintained. Seems like something got lost over the last generation: the basic knowledge of how to keep these windows in good repair.

When I got my hands on *Working Windows*, it was like a breath of fresh air! Finally, someone telling the truth and laying out the details about real windows in the real world! Terence Meany's candor in nailing bad painting as the number one enemy of wood windows was one of those moments where I found myself talking out loud, saying, "Hallelujah, someone has picked up on this!"

This book should also be praised for Terry's low-key wit and seasoned knowledge, both of which are a delight and a revelation. Most home repair books are not a very good "read." If they are well organized and well thought out, they can be useful, but rarely fun and funny. Few home repair problems can't benefit from a bit of dry wit, in my opinion. *Working Windows* is the best of the best—detailed and correct "how-to" advice, and at the same time readable and funny.

For years, I have had the idea that one day I would write the definitive book on the care and repair of wood windows. On one hand, I'm not overly pleased that Terry has beaten me to the punch here. On the other hand, the general public needs and deserves this book, and truly, I could not have written a better one.

—Mark A. Hetts, aka Mr. HandyPerson
San Francisco, 1998

PREFACE

What does a window do?

A window provides a link with and a view of the outside world. It's a source of light and ventilation as well as egress in case of emergencies. It can also be a source of frustration and expense in an older home if it is barely moving or inoperable.

I'm Mr. Window. I've repaired over three thousand windows of all types in the Seattle area. This book will share with you, the homeowner or curious carpenter, my practical knowledge of window repair. The information is both useful and realistic and can save you thousands of dollars in window replacement costs.

I am not a purist about old windows. You might just consider buying a new house with new windows (and doors, and bathrooms, a new roof, level floors, a new kitchen . . .) and leave this book for the next owner. But if it's Old World charm you want, I'll show you how to keep a big part of it.

In this guide, I'll explain repair techniques, describe tools and materials, and discuss the different types of windows found in most older buildings and homes. I'll limit the text to approximately pre-1950 wood windows.

These techniques really work! I've repaired some horrible windows and they're still in service today. The procedures in this book will produce both historically correct and practical working results at an affordable price. Follow them and you'll have operating, weathertight, and attractive, albeit quaint, windows of your own.

ACKNOWLEDGMENTS

This book was started more years ago than I care to admit. Several people have worked on the illustrations without which this would be a limited text indeed. I would like to thank Anita Lehmann, AIA, and Kathleen Rosales for their early help, Michael LaFond for the final drawings, and Mike Littaker for reviewing the text. Lastly, my thanks to Sandra Todd and Darlene Dubé at Todd/Dubé Graphics.

INTRODUCTION

Most of my work has been in homes and buildings built between 1890 and the late 1940s. The wood windows of this period include the following types:

- ✓ Double-hung (most common)
- ✓ Casement
- ✓ Awning
- ✓ Hopper
- ✓ Fixed
- ✓ Pivoting

Each type of window has advantages and disadvantages in terms of maintenance and operation, and will be described separately in the text.

Original window systems can often be improved through repairs and maintenance. You should consider a series of questions before beginning any work:

- ✓ Do I want all my windows to open?
- ✓ What are my safety and security considerations?
- ✓ If money is a concern, will I be in my home long enough to recoup my investment if I replace the windows?
- ✓ If comfort and quiet are my goals, and I am not concerned with keeping to the building's original architecture, should I even consider repairing rather than replacing with new insulated windows?
- ✓ If I do replace, what type of window should I purchase: aluminum, vinyl, or wood?
- ✓ Do I feel "handy" enough to do this work?

Home improvements often evolve around time and money, and windows are no exception. Even if you feel like you're "all thumbs," with practice you'll be able to do any repair technique described in this book without resorting to exotic tools or materials.

Start with a small window in a bedroom for practice and familiarize yourself with the techniques. Give yourself a day to complete the job. I think you'll be pleased with the results.

Please note: All prices quoted are effective as of this printing.

CHAPTER ONE

DOUBLE-HUNG WINDOWS

Double-hung windows have sash that slide up and down. They look like this:

Upper Sash

Lower Sash

DIAGRAM I

The following diagrams give the real names of actual parts of the window (instead of, "Oh, you know, that little wheel thingy that the rope goes through").

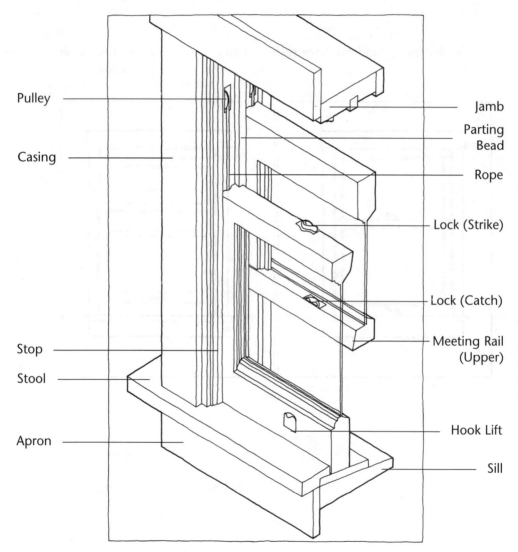

DIAGRAM 2

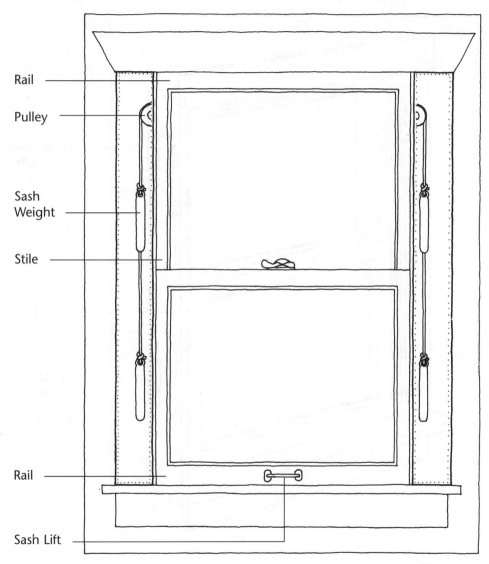

Rail

Pulley

Sash
Weight

Stile

Rail

Sash Lift

DIAGRAM 3

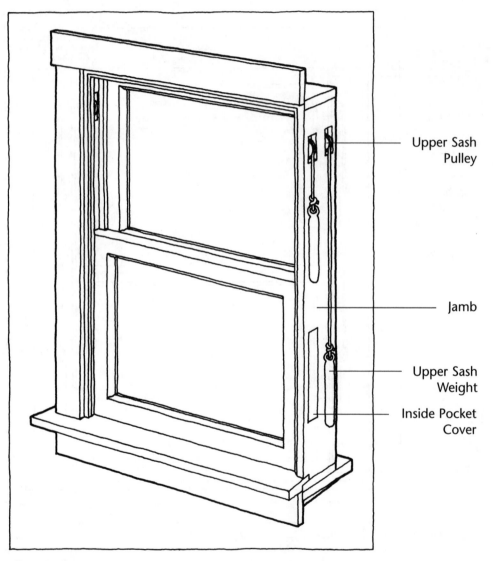

Upper Sash
Pulley

Jamb

Upper Sash
Weight

Inside Pocket
Cover

Diagram 4

THE DETAILS

✓ The sash is the section that moves and holds the glass. It consists of two horizontal pieces called rails and two vertical pieces called stiles.
✓ The jamb is the larger window frame in which the sash slide.
✓ The weights counterbalance the sash so they remain open.
✓ The pulleys facilitate the sliding.
✓ The pocket covers provide access to the weights.
✓ The parting beads separate the upper and lower sash so they can slide past each other.
✓ The interior stop and the blind stop hold the sash in place.
✓ The casings are the wood trim that set the window in place and stabilize it. On brick and stucco buildings, the exterior trim is usually brick molding.

What? You don't have pulleys or pocket covers? Don't worry, I'll cover those windows, too.

TYPICAL PROBLEMS

✓ Sash are painted shut.
✓ Ropes are broken or frayed.
✓ Paint and putty have deteriorated.
✓ Hardware is broken or missing.
✓ Glass is cracked.
✓ Window is not weathertight.
✓ Wood is rotted or damaged.

Once upon a time, in a land far away, all windows opened. Then the painters came and that was the end of that. Before attempting to open your windows, you must determine:

✓ Are they weather-stripped?
✓ Do they have pulleys?
✓ What kind of pulleys do they have?

WEATHER STRIPPING

There are several types of weather stripping, but the most common used with old windows is called interlocking weather stripping. This is a hindrance to work around, especially if the window is painted shut. Diagrams 5 and 6 show a typical section of this material. If your window is painted shut, look outside under the bottom corners of the upper sash. If you see a 1- to 2-inch section of metal sticking out and nailed to the jamb, then you, too, have this weather stripping.

Note: Sometimes, the weather stripping does not extend down at the corners. You'll have to look carefully for the end of the weather stripping. Usually, some windows in the house open and you can then tell if they are weather-stripped. Often, if one was done, most or all of the others were also done.

Interlocking weather stripping is fitted into a channel (a groove) that is cut into three sides of each sash. It is also fitted at the meeting rail (where the upper and lower sash lock together) and must line up precisely in order for the window to slide and lock properly.

There are some variations of this material. One type has a piece nailed to the sash itself, which then slides into the piece nailed to the jamb. Installing interlocking material is quite an art and is rarely done today. This weather stripping is usually salvageable and I recommend reinstalling it when possible. Interlocking weather stripping is discussed in more detail on pages 43–45.

PULLEYS

Next, determine if you have pulleys, which is simple enough to do. You will have either the wheel type or a duplex pulley. Duplex pulleys and sash balances were introduced in the 1940s. An example of each is shown in Diagrams 7 and 8.

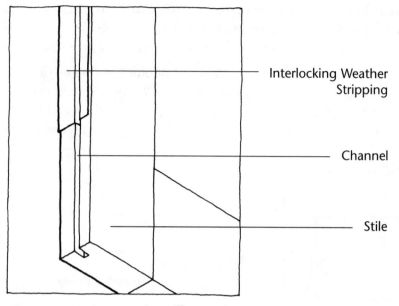

Interlocking Weather Stripping

Channel

Stile

DIAGRAM 5

Top View

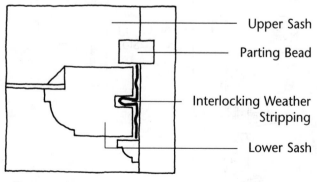

Upper Sash

Parting Bead

Interlocking Weather Stripping

Lower Sash

DIAGRAM 6

A duplex pulley is a metal box, installed in the jamb, containing spring-wound cables. One end of a cable is attached to the lower corner or corners of each sash. A large window will have two duplex pulleys. The cables are prone to snapping if they are not removed carefully.

If you do not have duplex pulleys and do not have standard pulleys and do not have sash pins (see Diagrams 9 and 10), then *stop!* The builder never intended this window to open. Usually, you'll find this in a group of three to four or more double-hung windows where only

Duplex Pulley

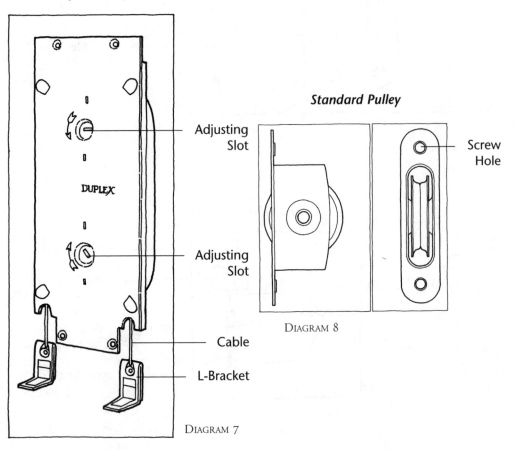

Adjusting Slot

DUPLEX

Adjusting Slot

Cable

L-Bracket

Standard Pulley

Screw Hole

DIAGRAM 8

DIAGRAM 7

the end ones or every other one will open. Those smart builders probably saved, oh, three to four dollars a window installing them without pulleys and weights.

These windows may still need repairs. If so, follow the repair instructions for double-hung windows.

If you really want a fixed window to open, see Chapter 3.

Note: There are replacement pulleys that use a self-winding steel tape instead of ropes and weights. I would stick with the original system when possible since it's simple and can almost always be repaired.

SASH PINS

Okay, what are sash pins? They are spring-loaded pins installed into the sides of the sash in lieu of ropes and weights. When the sash is raised and the pins released, the ends of the pins insert into holes in the jamb, which have been drilled at different heights, like every 6 inches or so. This prevents the sash from dropping. They do the job and replacement pins are still manufactured. These are also called guillotine windows, for obvious reasons.

Pins may be stuck due to paint buildup and you may have to twist and pull them loose with a vise grips or pliers. If a pin is damaged and needs to be replaced, tap the end near the glass gently with a hammer. Each pin is held in by friction (the metal casing pushes against the drilled hole the pin sits in). As it's forced out of the hole, you'll be able to grab the other end with pliers and twist it out completely. If you're replacing one, you may as well replace both of them. Sash pins are not a common hardware item and may have to be ordered. Some older, been-in-town-forever types of hardware stores might have them in stock, so call around.

For more regarding opening windows with sash pins, see page 13.

Sash Pin

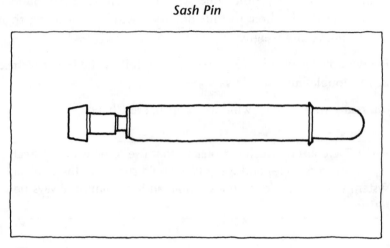

Diagram 9

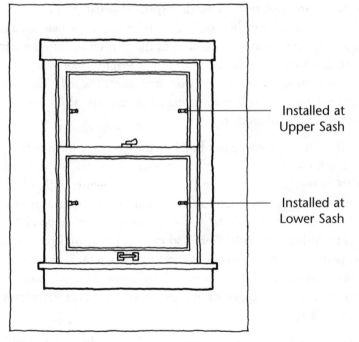

Installed at
Upper Sash

Installed at
Lower Sash

Diagram 10

OPENING THE WINDOW

All you want to do is get the lower sash open. You don't have any weather stripping. You can have either type of pulley; it doesn't matter at this point.

Beware: Sometimes the bottom rails are quite loose and can drop off when you open the sash. The glass may also be loose. Hold on to or otherwise secure these while opening the sash. If the glass is badly cracked, be absolutely sure to tape the cracks, preferably on both sides! This prevents the glass from falling out while you remove the sash.

Warning! The sash may be nailed or screwed shut. This is more likely if the window is in an area vulnerable to break-ins. I have also found that old school buildings have some windows nailed shut to prevent kids from doing whatever kids would do at an open window. The nails are inevitably on the interior side. If your windows are stained and varnished, and thus unpainted, and you can't budge the sash using the techniques described below, slide a stiff blade putty knife between the vertical stiles and the jamb. If you hit an obstruction, pry the two apart slightly and see if it's a nail. If so, force the end of the putty knife against the nail and hammer it until the nail either breaks or bends loose from the jamb. If it's a screw, try to find the head and unscrew it. Otherwise, cut the shaft of the screw with a hacksaw blade or reciprocating saw (a power saw with a reciprocating blade, like an electric knife for meat carving). The stops will have to be removed (as will the parting beads if you're pulling the upper sash out).

If the upper sash is nailed shut, the nails are often under its lower two corners on the exterior section of the jamb. Usually, I find the heads sticking out enough to make them noticeable and they can then be pulled with a vise grips or small crowbar.

To open the sash, you have to break the paint seal on all four sides. You can do this by using a wide, sharp, chisel-type putty knife and hammer; a heat gun; or chemical paint remover.

The putty knife and hammer are the least messy, although these will not remove the paint, only break the seal, which is normally all that's necessary. The heat gun or paint remover will remove much of the excess paint, but will require a lot of cleanup and repainting.

The diagram below shows where the paint must be broken or removed. This is an interior view. For best results, break the paint on both sides if possible.

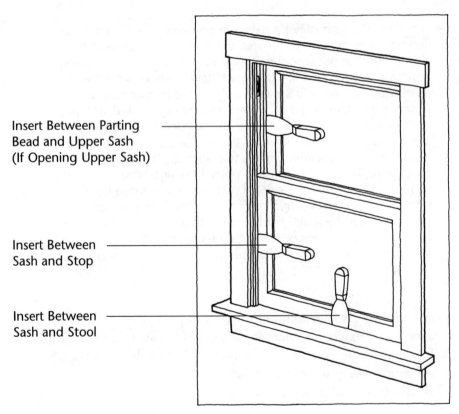

Insert Between Parting
Bead and Upper Sash
(If Opening Upper Sash)

Insert Between
Sash and Stop

Insert Between
Sash and Stool

DIAGRAM 11

If you are using a putty knife, break the paint on both the inside and outside of the sash. Then insert the knife under the bottom rail of the sash, between it and the sill, and pry upward.

Check that the lock is open! You might spray some silicone or WD-40 on the jamb first so the sash will slide more easily. If you have used a heat gun or chemical remover, insert the putty knife here as well and force the sash up. *Don't use a screwdriver!* This will work, but it will gouge the wood.

Warning! Don't push up on the upper rail of the lower sash and try to force the sash up. If you push hard enough, you can loosen the rail or even break it at the corners. Pushing up at the middle of the rail can loosen the glass. The meeting rail is fairly narrow, more a function of aesthetics than practicality, and is particularly tenuous on large sash. This also holds true when opening the upper sash: Don't push down in the middle of the lower rail. It's okay to push down in the corners after the sash is freely moving.

If the sash will barely budge, or if you cannot access the outside and get a putty knife between the bottom rail and the sill, then you will have to remove the stops. The easiest way to do this is shown in Diagram 12. You can also skip the preceding steps and open the sash by removing the stops. This is particularly useful when the windows are on the second story or higher and you can't break the paint on the exterior.

If you have sash pins, loosen the pins and pull them out as far as they will come. Wedge a sliver of wood between the pin and its casing so the pins will not lock into the jamb. This way, you can loosen the sash and pull it forward and out. If you have four hands (one for each pin and one each for the hammer and putty knife) you can ignore this advice. My perspective is written for someone bravely and courageously doing the work alone, keeping America number one in window restoration. It is simply coincidental that Mr. Window matches this description.

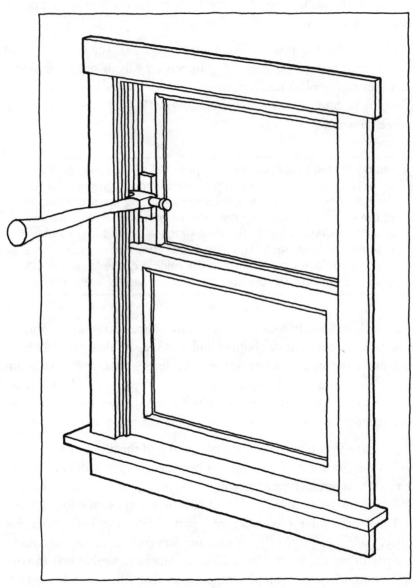

DIAGRAM 12

After you have loosened the stop with the claw end of a hammer, finish the job with a small crowbar or stiff putty knife. Bend the stop out a little at a time so it doesn't crack. With both stops removed, carefully insert the putty knife between the upper and lower sash at the meeting rail. Remember, the sash lock together at a slight angle, so don't try to hammer the putty knife straight down.

Tap it with a hammer until the two sash separate, then work along the length of the meeting rail. You don't have to tap too hard, so take your time. Pull the sash toward you and work it back and forth several times until it breaks free and can be raised. Don't pull one end out at too much of an angle before freeing the entire length of the sash! You can stress and bend the glass, and it can crack. Remember, note if the glass or bottom rail is loose as you raise it and secure it as you go.

The meeting rail may be full of caulk or spackle. If this is the case, you may have to be more aggressive when tapping the putty knife.

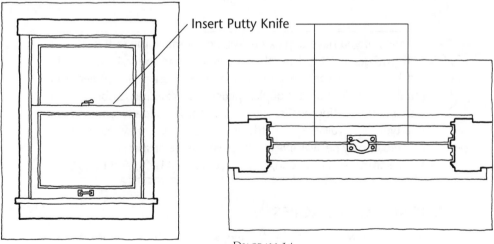

Insert Putty Knife

DIAGRAM 13

DIAGRAM 14

Be careful with the old ropes! If they are covered with a lot of paint, they will be stiff and prone to break if moved too abruptly. Slowly work the sash up and down until the paint breaks and the rope moves through the pulley. Even if there isn't much paint buildup, old ropes are typically made of cotton and can be weak, but still serviceable. Replacement is always a good idea and I recommend it.

The edges of the stops and the sash will probably be caked with paint. The longer it's been painted shut the more often it's been painted as a rule. Scrape off the excess paint before reinstalling. For complete stripping, see pages 59–66.

INSTALLING THE STOPS

When reinstalling the stops, allow enough room between them and the sash so it will slide easily. I usually line them up, partially hammer one nail at about the center of the stop, and then raise the sash and check for adjustment before nailing the rest of it. A good way of spacing is to insert a flexible (not stiff) putty knife between the sash and the stop and use this as a guide. If the sash is tight or sticking, spray the jamb and the area where the sash runs against the stop with lubricant.

Warning! If you have duplex pulleys, slowly move the sash back and forth and gently lift it. The cables are attached to the sash via small L-brackets. These can be corroded and may snap if handled too roughly. Installing a new duplex pulley requires disassembling both sash and the parting beads. These pulleys are a specialty item and are not typically available at hardware stores. They may have to be ordered or may be available at a large wholesale or specialty hardware store. For more information, please see pages 41–43, and page 84.

REPLACING THE ROPES

If your window has standard pulleys (rather than duplex pulleys), then either rope or sash chain can be used to attach the sash to the weights. Sash chain is costlier than rope and was most often used with very heavy sash, in industrial buildings, or in expensive homes and apartments.

Although pure-cotton sash rope is still sold, a blend of cotton and synthetic material is a better choice since it is stronger and more durable. It is sold by number (#7, #8, etc.), which indicates its diameter. Number 8 rope is more than sufficient for most uses, certainly for residential use. If it isn't available at a local hardware store, try a rope supplier (listed in the Yellow Pages). One hundred percent synthetic rope is okay, but harder to work with. The ends can fray and may have to be sealed by burning them with a small flame.

You can rope either the lower sash alone or both the upper and lower sash. We'll start with the lower sash.

Lower Sash Rope Replacement and Pocket Covers

With the sash removed, look for a pocket cover. Pocket covers are found in one of two locations. If your house was built roughly prior to 1900, the pocket cover may be cut into the exterior portion of the jamb; that is, where the upper sash slides down, about 6 inches from the sill. If the window has been painted a couple of hundred times, it may be hard to see the outline of the cover. Diagrams 15–17 show this cover.

A small screw secures the bottom of the cover to the jamb. Like the top, the bottom end is cut at a 45-degree angle. The top end has two notches cut into it that wedge against two nails in the jamb as shown in Diagram 17. To remove the cover, break the paint on its two vertical sides with a putty knife or score with the edge of a sharp blade. Remove the screw (if it doesn't come out, just loosen it), and slowly pry the cover out starting near the bottom.

You can remove the cover by 1) wedging a stiff putty knife between the parting bead and the cover and, alternately, between the exterior blind stop and the cover, forcing it out; or 2) inserting a narrow, thin putty

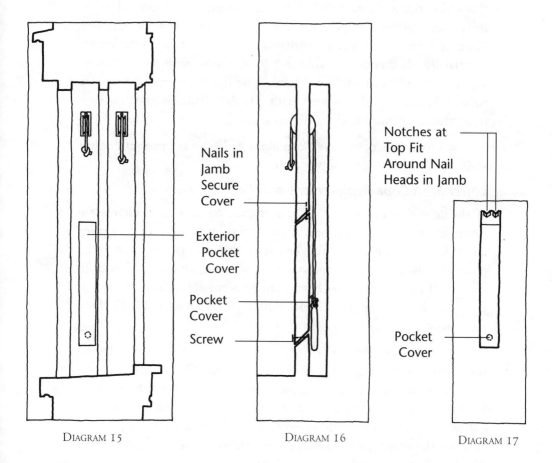

Nails in
Jamb
Secure
Cover

Exterior
Pocket
Cover

Pocket
Cover

Screw

Notches at
Top Fit
Around Nail
Heads in Jamb

Pocket
Cover

DIAGRAM 15

DIAGRAM 16

DIAGRAM 17

knife at the bottom edge of the pocket cover (remember to follow the angle here) and slowly forcing it out and down. Once it's a little loose from either method you can then pull it out the rest of the way. Combining both methods is often best.

With the cover removed, you should see one or both of the window weights at the bottom of the pocket. Either way, you have a problem. The weight from the upper sash can block your easy access to the weight from the lower sash (while the upper sash is closed or in the up position, its weight will be at the bottom of the pocket or close to it). If both the ropes are broken, the weights may be tightly wedged. If both sash are the same size, you can always attach the rope for the lower sash to either weight, whichever is most accessible. If they're different sizes, you'll have to use the correct weight. If you're going to rerope both sash, then the upper weight can be moved out of the way when the sash is removed by pulling on its old rope. If not, this can be a bit difficult if room is tight.

Although it's rare with an exterior pocket cover, your home or building may have wood or metal dividers separating the weights. These dividers are attached to the top of the weight pocket and loosely hang down the length of the pocket to keep the weights apart. If you have one of these and are attempting to rerope the lower sash only, you will have to get the weight for the upper sash out of the way. You can either cut the weight from its rope and remove it, try to force it up toward the pulley, or open the upper sash and pull the weight up completely. If the divider is made out of wood, you can always snap off the bottom 12 inches or so, but this doesn't always provide enough access to the lower sash weight. If the dividers are metal, attempting to bend them and cut them off usually results in a small mess. With these, you're better off opening the upper sash.

If the weights are jammed, try forcing a large screwdriver or crowbar between the weights and shifting them around until you can attach the rope. Spraying them with a lot of lubricant can help. Let loose with the WD-40. If they are wedged too tight to move in any direction, you'll have to take the casing off and access them from the front.

Hey, wait a minute, Mr. Window, I pulled off the pocket cover between two of my windows and all I could see were two big weights with a little wheel pulley thingy wired to the top of each one. Other than possibly being a suspected FBI listening device, as are many other items in my house, what's the deal? I don't get it.

These are not FBI listening devices, although you might take a second look at your doorbell chimes. Two side-by-side double-hung windows will share one pocket for their respective weights. If the pocket is too narrow to hold four weights (one for each upper sash and one for each lower sash), a single weight will be used, commensurately heavy enough to counterbalance two sash. In order for this trick to work, a small pulley is attached with baling wire to the hole at the top of the weight and a single rope is passed through it and attached to both sash as shown in Diagram 18. I'll explain how to rerope these windows on page 24.

Let's assume the cover is removed and you have plenty of room (ha-ha-ha). How do you get the rope down the wall? Well, you could try feeding it through and down the pulley by itself and, hope springing eternal, believe that the end will drop right to the bottom. Or you could do what Mr. Window does: Get a small piece of chain (like plumber's chain or sash chain), attach a wire twist (like those that come with plastic trash bags) to one end, and then wrap the other end of the twist around the end of the rope. Drop the chain down through the pulley and then feed the rope through. Seconds later, the rope will reach your eagerly awaiting hand, unless it gets hung up on something and then you may have to feed it through again. You particularly don't want it to get wrapped around the rope for the other sash. Cut

Side-by-Side Sash Sharing Weight, Center Pocket

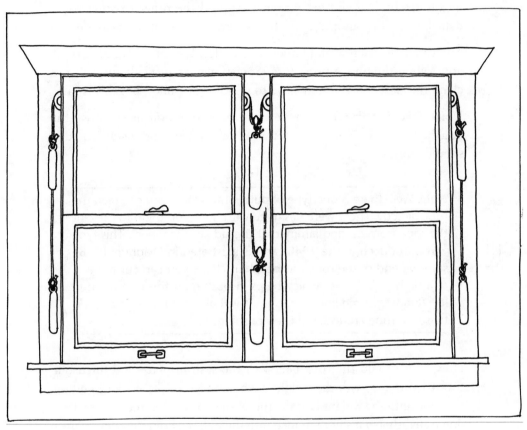

Diagram 18

the old rope away from the weight and attach the new rope. With the weight at the bottom of the pocket, cut the rope about 6 inches out from the pulley and knot the end. Tug on the weight a few times to be sure the knot is tight. Move the weight up and down to check that it moves freely. If it did get wrapped around the other existing rope, detach it, pull it out and up to the pulley, and feed it down again.

You can also unscrew and remove the pulley, but this is unnecessary if you follow the above procedure. Sometimes it's difficult to push the chain through and you may have to remove the pulley, but this is rare.

Don't have a chain? Try a piece of string with a bolt or small weight attached to it. As long as it fits through the pulley and it's weighted it should work.

Note: Well, there is one type of pulley into which you can feed the rope directly. These were designed with hoods on them to prevent the rope from getting jammed at the side of the wheel. This type was introduced in the 1940s and is illustrated in Diagram 19. Be sure the end of the rope has been cut clean; you can cut the end at a slight angle, too, which helps in pushing it through the pulley. Rubbing some liquid soap on it will also help. If it gets stuck, twist the rope around and keep pushing.

How long should the rope be? With the sash in place and tilted out toward you and with the weight at the bottom of the pocket, pull on the rope until the weight is at the top of the pocket. Let the weight drop down slightly (so it's not jammed into the pulley), hold the rope against the side of the sash at the knot hole, and then cut it about 4 to 5 inches beyond the hole. Tie an overhand knot (for all you nonknot types, it's the first knot you form when tying your shoes; if you only wear loafers, you're out of luck) at the end of the rope and force it into the hole. If the hole is small or not holding the rope securely, hammer a small nail through the knot and into the sash. Nail it at an angle to be sure it does not go through and strike the edge of the glass.

Hooded Pulley

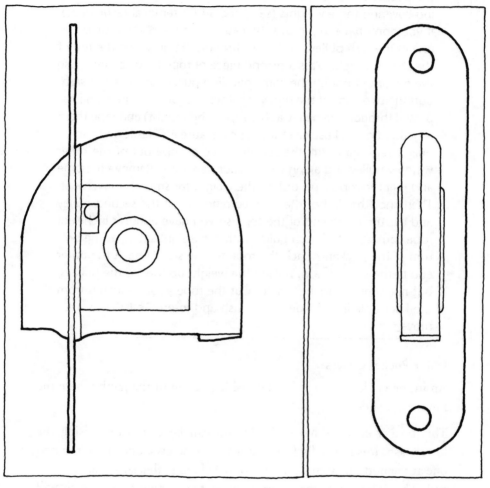

DIAGRAM 19

Hey, what about those shared weights with the pulleys at the top of them? If the tops of these weights are too far above the top of the pocket cover for you to reach, you'll have to remove the casing covering these weights (see page 34 for removal techniques). If you don't have to remove the casing, then pass the rope down one of the sash pulleys and then through the pulley on the top of the shared weight. Pass a second piece of rope (you can even use the old one) through the corresponding pulley for the other sash. Butt the two ends of the ropes together (be sure your new one has passed through the pulley at the top of the weight) and tape them together tightly. I use electrical tape because it's elastic and can be pulled very tight. Pull the second piece of rope out of the other window pulley and along with it your new rope. Remove the tape and pull the rope taut, testing the weight for smooth movement. Then knot the end of the rope coming out of the second pulley and cut the other end of the rope so you have about 4 inches of rope coming out of each pulley with the weight sitting at the bottom of the pocket. Attach the rope to one sash. Attach the other end to the second sash, pulling the weight up toward the pulleys, but not jammed against them. Cut the rope about 6 inches from the knot hole in the side of the sash and insert. Test the sash for movement.

Inside Pocket Covers

An inside pocket cover is on the inside portion of the jamb where the lower sash slides.

This pocket cover is more visible and can be seen after raising the lower sash. It is normally fastened with two screws, one at the top and one at the bottom. Sometimes it is only held in with a small nail at each end. The outer lip of the cover is under the parting bead, which will have to be pried out slightly in order to remove the cover.

Start at the bottom of the parting bead using a stiff putty knife. Break the paint on both sides and slowly bend the bead out. You'll have to stop short of the upper sash; otherwise, the bead will break. After it has been loosened and pulled out a ways, put a small block of wood between the end of the bead and the jamb to keep it away from the pocket cover. Then unscrew the cover and pry it out at the bottom, gradually pulling it down and out. Install the new rope and tie on to the weight.

Inside Pocket Cover

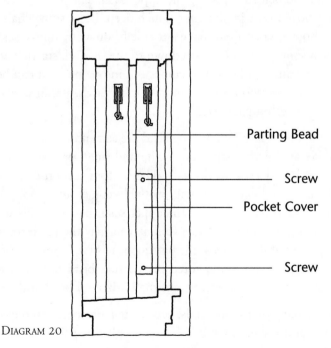

Parting Bead

Screw

Pocket Cover

Screw

DIAGRAM 20

While the sash is removed, it is an opportune time to strip off or sand the paint and repaint, replace any broken glass or putty, and install weather stripping. Please see Chapter 4 for the details of this work.

REMOVING BOTH SASH, REPLACING THE PARTING BEADS

Not satisfied to leave well enough alone, you've decided to pull out the upper sash and make it operable as well. This offers an opportunity for minor destruction, which has its moments. Why bother with the upper sash? Improved ventilation, for one thing. Also, the meeting rails can be painted and you won't have to look at years of drips and runs from past paint jobs. And it's just kind of cool to pull the upper sash down.

After removing the lower sash, it will be necessary to remove the parting bead before removing the upper sash. The parting bead is seated in a groove in the jamb about ⅜-inch deep. If, by some chance, the winds of homeowners' fate have provided you with upper sash that open, then simply lower the sash down to the sill and, starting at the top, pry the parting bead out. If it comes out in one piece, it can be reused, but as it's a common item at most lumberyards, it can easily be replaced (note sizes on page 31).

If the upper sash and parting bead are cemented in with paint, then chip away at it with a stiff putty knife and small pry bar. I've found that a small WonderBar works well. The bottom section of the parting bead (behind the lower sash) will probably come out in one piece and then snap off at the bottom of the upper sash. Be aggressive with the upper section, but not so aggressive that you mar the jamb too much. Break the paint at the edges of the parting bead first. Hammer the straight end of the pry bar in and force the parting bead out. You only have to remove the vertical pieces, not the horizontal bead at the header.

After removing both beads, break the paint between the outside of the sash and the exterior blind stop on all three sides. Place a stiff putty knife at the lower outside corners, tap it with a hammer, and pry the sash forward. Grab the bottom and work it back and forth, pulling it down at the same time.

> *Note:* As you remove the parting beads and break the upper sash loose, it may fall suddenly if its ropes are broken, so be prepared to catch it. If it is a large sash, nail a couple of wood blocks on to the jamb, a few inches under the bottom rail, to catch the sash if it begins to move.

It's best to break the outside paint seal, especially if it's been caulked. If you can't break all of the paint seal outside, break it as far as you can reach and work the sash back and forth, pulling down slightly. *Do this while holding the corners, not the middle of the lower rail!* Remove the sash and install the ropes.

If you have a tall window, you can attach a stiff putty knife to the end of a board, such as a 2-by-2, and carefully tap it to break the paint seal. Screw and tape the putty knife tightly to the wood; if you're working several stories up, drill a hole in the other end of the board, tie a rope through it, and loop the rest of the rope around your wrist in case you drop your new tool on someone below.

> *Note:* The easiest way to figure out the right rope length is to just give yourself 6 inches or so of extra length out of the pulley. Cut the rope, knot it, and pull the weight up to the top of the pulley. Wrap the rope around an old piece of rope or scrap of cardboard so the weight stays up. This way, one weight is not in the way of the other at the bottom of the pocket when you're measuring the remaining ropes. This is especially helpful if you have two windows side by side with four weights in a shared pocket and several of the old ropes have snapped.

You have to get the weights clear of each other. This wastes a small amount of rope, but it's not like the entire ozone layer will be destroyed because you threw out a couple of feet of rope. Also, if you're working on very tall windows, which require a ladder to get at the pulleys, it's really helpful to pull the weights up and out of the way and wrap the ropes near the pulley as noted above. This way, you will have all four ropes dangling in front of you while you're standing on the floor and installing the sash rather than having to balance the sash and yourself on a ladder while grabbing the rope out of the pulley. See, tall windows are usually *heavy* windows and they always have *pedestrians* right underneath, three or four stories below, looking up, and having the following conversation:

> *"Huh, guess they're fixing those windows, huh?"*
>
> *"Yeah, sure looks like it."*
>
> *"What do ya think would happen if they dropped one of those, huh? Bet it'd really hurt."*
>
> *"Uh, yeah, bet it would. That's right."*

Believe me, it's a lot easier dealing with this from the floor than from a ladder.

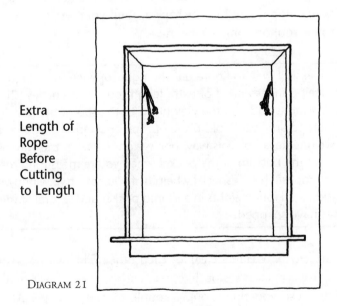

Extra Length of Rope Before Cutting to Length

DIAGRAM 21

DIAGRAM 22

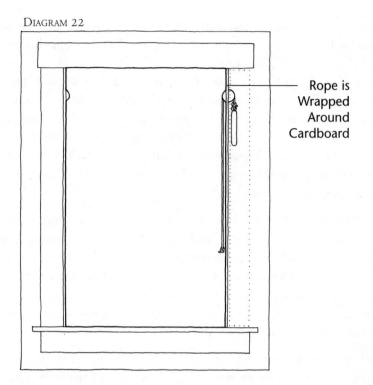

Rope is
Wrapped
Around
Cardboard

The lengths for the upper ropes have to be exact or the weights will hit the bottom of the pocket before the sash is closed all the way. To determine the length, place the sash on the stool, pull the weights up tight to the pulley, and cut the rope about 2 to 3 inches from the knot hole, knot it, and place the knot in the hole. Slide the sash all the way up and be sure it closes tightly (and without its weights hitting the lower sash weights; these should be up and out of the way). If it does drop open, check inside the pocket to see if the weights have hit the bottom. If they have, then shorten the ropes. If they haven't, and the sash still doesn't close, then the weights are too light. You can do one of the following:

✓ Add some weight.
✓ Weather-strip the sash (this often tightens it up sufficiently).
✓ Add a sash control to one or both sides.

How do you add weight? Just about anything that can fit around the rope will do. Large washers, old gears, etc. Put the rope through them first and then tie it on to the weight. Or, if you're adding something that won't fit around the rope, you can add to the bottom of the weight by wrapping baling wire around it and then your additional weight to the other end of the wire. I wrap the wire around the weight, cinch it tightly, and then wrap it all with several layers of electrical tape or duct tape. It may not look very elegant, but it works. One time, with nothing else available, I taped a small rock to a weight. It did the job and was, like, very organic.

Scrap metal salvage yards may have old window weights. Some architectural salvage specialty shops have them as well. Contractors usually throw old weights away when remodeling if they're tearing into the walls and replacing the windows. Grab some of these if you need heavier weights. Also, contact a company that installs new windows and inquire if you can procure some weights from one of their jobs after the old windows are removed.

What are sash controls? They're pieces of spring metal, sold in pairs, used in place of broken ropes. The movement of the sash won't be as smooth as with ropes, but they do provide a quick fix. They can also be used to supplement ropes when the sash is too heavy for the existing weights. This sometimes happens when the glass has been changed and a heavier piece added, such as security glass or translucent glass in a bathroom (for privacy). You may only need one control or even half of one (cut lengthwise).

Once the upper sash is secured and happy, install the old parting bead or cut a new one to length and install it. How? Lower the sash to the sill or as close as it will go, then poke the end of the parting bead in between the corner of the sash (at the bottom rail, which has been notched to accommodate the parting bead) and the jamb. Work it in all the way to the top, tapping a block of wood against it with a hammer to secure it. Note that the end of the parting bead that sits on the sill is cut at a slight angle to accommodate the slope of the sill. If you install a new parting bead, you may have to plane or sand down the two edges going into the groove for a smooth fit.

Note: Parting beads come in several different sizes. The most common, and usually available, is ¾ inch by ½ inch. Other quaint sizes include ¾ inch by ⅜ inch and ⅞ inch by ⅜ inch. Unless you want to have these nonstandard sizes milled, you'll have to work around what's available.

You can fake the ⅜-inch figure by planing or sanding down the edge of a ¾-inch-by-½-inch parting bead. The ⅞-inch-by-⅜-inch is a little

Sash Controls

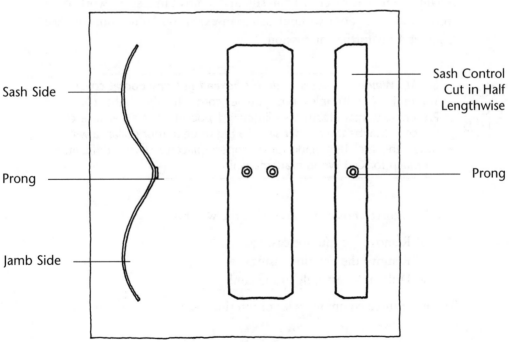

DIAGRAM 23

tougher. You can take a ¾-inch-by-½-inch, slightly plane down the ½-inch dimension, stuff it into the jamb until it stops, secure it with small wire nails, and call it good. It usually will fill out for most of the extra needed ⅛ inch. Of course, Mr. Window would never consider doing anything like this. Also, not all ¾-inch-by-½-inch parting beads are the same size. They will vary with different suppliers. They can be undersize to some degree. Another sign of sliding standards and increased cost of raw materials, I suppose. Find a lumberyard that carries material truer to the stated dimensions.

Slide the upper sash up and down a few times for good measure. If the parting bead sticks out too much, put your block of wood on it and hammer a bit more. It should be uniform its entire length. Then install the lower sash and the stops.

Again, while the sash are out, you have an opportunity to strip and repaint them. The exterior trim, sill, and jambs can also be worked on from inside the room without using an extension ladder outside. See Chapter 4 for further discussion.

So, Mr. Window, what do I do if I haven't got any pocket covers? You're in *big* trouble, but you've come to the right place. Presumably, manufacturers eliminated pocket covers because of the cost. Maybe the builder saved a big three to four dollars a window here, too, but made future rope replacement very difficult. So much for Old World craftsmanship.

You have three choices for accessing the weights:

- ✓ Remove the interior casings.
- ✓ Remove the exterior casings.
- ✓ Drill an access hole in the jamb.

There are three common styles of interior casings:

- ✓ Vertical casings that butt up against an upper horizontal casing
- ✓ Vertical casings that are miter-cut at a 45-degree angle against the upper casing and often have an additional piece of trim (a backband) around the outer edge
- ✓ Vertical casings butted to a horizontal casing with a backband around the edge

Common Casing Styles

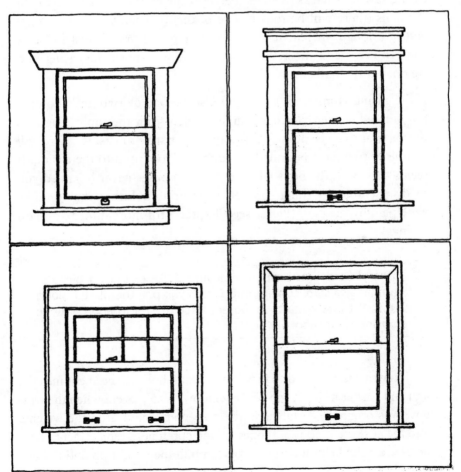

DIAGRAM 24

As a broad guideline, windows with mitered casings (usually from the 1920s and later) are less likely to have pocket covers, although this isn't an absolute. These casings are also a bit more difficult to remove.

The easiest way to remove either type, after the stops are removed, is to insert a stiff putty knife between the casing and the jamb and slowly pry out against the casing. After working your way up to the top, and having moved the casing out ½ inch or so, insert a reciprocating saw or a hacksaw blade between the casing and jamb and cut the nails (there will be four to five of them). Then stuff the straight end of a long crowbar in under the casing and pry against its other edge, which sits against the plaster. Gradually push the casing out. Again, cut the nails.

If the casing is mitered, there will also be one or two nails holding the mitered corner together, usually nailed from the top casing into the vertical casings. Sometimes, with either style of casing, there will be one or two nails pounded through the stool up into the casing. It seems clear that the boys who built these houses never intended you to disassemble anything, broken rope or not. Either that or they were paid by the nail. (Please see Chapter 5 for more information on casings.)

Warning! Sometimes, when removing these casings, a piece of lath may also start coming out, which will pull the plaster along with it. If the lath starts to loosen, force it back in and continue removing the casing.

With the casing removed, you will find that a hole has been cut into the lath and plaster near the top of the window. This was cut when the window was originally installed so the carpenters could drop the weights into the pockets. If your old ropes are intact but need replacement, these holes are quite helpful because you can pull the weight up and remove it, feed a new rope through the pulley, and easily attach it to the weight. If the weights are stuck at the bottom of the pocket, you will have to cut away the lath and plaster at the top of the weight and drop your rope down. Chop out a small bit of plaster a foot or so from the bottom and push a narrow putty knife through between the lath. If you hit the weight, remove the lath from that point upward until you have exposed the top of the weight. If you cannot feel the weight, then cut down from that point.

If your casings are the butted type (without the backband), you may find after removal that the whole pocket is exposed and that the plaster and lath were not run all the way to the jamb. This will be the case if the house was built, approximately, prior to 1920. Houses built in the 1920s and thereafter usually had the plaster and lath installed right up to the jamb.

There are always variations. You may have wood walls covered with wallpaper and no plaster at all. You may have had a replacement window installed without pocket covers and with plywood covering the pocket under the casing. I have tried to describe the most common situations.

EXTERIOR CASINGS AND BRICK MOLDING

There are some circumstances when you don't want to remove the interior casings. They may sit against expensive wallpaper or you may want to limit the amount of repainting you'll have to do. You may then want to consider other approaches.

If you have exterior wood siding, you will probably have wide casings, similar in size to your interior ones or wider. Pry them off and the whole pocket will be exposed. I particularly recommend removing them if they are weathered, since they come off fairly easily.

These may also have nails coming up through the sill securing them. If you have brick molding (on either brick or stucco buildings), you will have a blind stop about 3½ inches wide under the molding. This will necessitate drilling or cutting an access hole through the stop in order to install the ropes. Again, you will probably have nails going through the sills and into the brick molding. Think twice before removing this.

ACCESS HOLES

Easier yet (with brick molding) is to drill an access hole into the jamb. With both sash removed (or even just the lower if you are only replacing its ropes), you will need to determine where the top of the weights are (their distance from the bottom of the pocket). How? Well, usually at least one of the ropes is intact. If so, and assuming the rope as it comes out of the pulley has a little slack, pull the rope so it is barely tight, pinch the section coming right out of the pulley, and pull it until the weight is at the pulley. Where your

Exterior View: Sill Nailed Up and into Casings

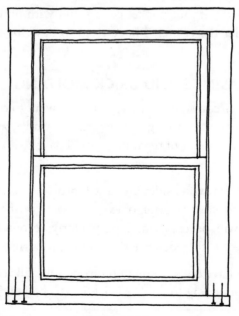

DIAGRAM 25

fingers meet the jamb will give you an approximate location for the top of the weight (see Diagram 26).

If the ropes are tight at the pulleys, it means that their length does not allow the weights to hit the bottom of the pocket, and even if you pull them out and measure to the jamb you will have to guess as to where to drill your hole. In either case, drill an inch or two higher than you expect the top of the weight to be found. If you have two different sizes of sash, drill for the top of the heavier, and thus taller, weight.

How to drill? You can use a 1-inch to 1¼-inch spade bit or a hole saw. Drill one hole and feel around for the top of the weights. If the weights have jammed up on top of each other you'll have to free them from each other by prying them apart with a large screwdriver or other tool.

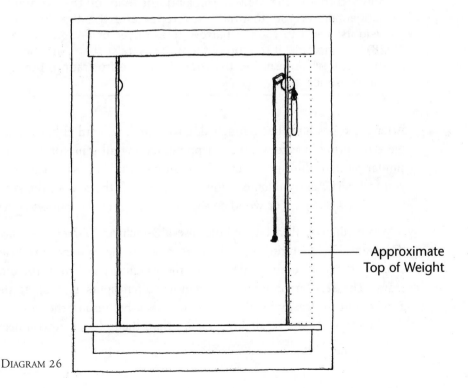

Approximate
Top of Weight

DIAGRAM 26

The first hole will determine where to locate the second hole. If you are too high (above the top of the weight), drill one lower. If too low, drill higher. If you have a space between these holes (this space should be 2 inches or so), remove this section of the jamb by chiseling it out or sawing it. You will now have a rough oval-shaped opening through which you can attach the new ropes.

Hold on, Mr. Window. I did this and the hole is small and a nuisance to deal with. I agree. This takes longer than using real pocket covers. If you're trying not to tear off the casings, though, and cannot access the weights from the exterior, then you haven't much choice. I find that a small piece of baling wire or a section of a metal clothes hanger is useful for moving the weights around and hooking the rope after it's been dropped down through the pulley. Hooking the end of the wire or hanger allows you to grab stray ropes and the tops of the weights. You can force a narrow screwdriver or awl (Diagram 28) into the hole at the top of the weights, raise them, and hold them still while inserting the rope. It can be frustrating, but it can be done.

After the ropes have been attached, cover the hole with either a small piece of spring bronze weather-stripping, nailing all four corners, or a similar piece of thin sheet metal. This allows future access if needed. If you feel particularly talented, you can square off the hole in the jamb and insert a custom-cut wood cover, similar to a regular pocket cover.

If you want to drill a larger hole, use a 3-inch or 3½-inch hole saw (Diagram 27), centering your hole on a scrap piece of parting bead stuck in the groove above the top of the weight as shown in the diagram. The section of jamb you remove often splits in half at the groove, but can easily be glued together. Also, because of the saw cut, the section will now be slightly smaller than the hole where you need

Removing Plug with a Hole Saw

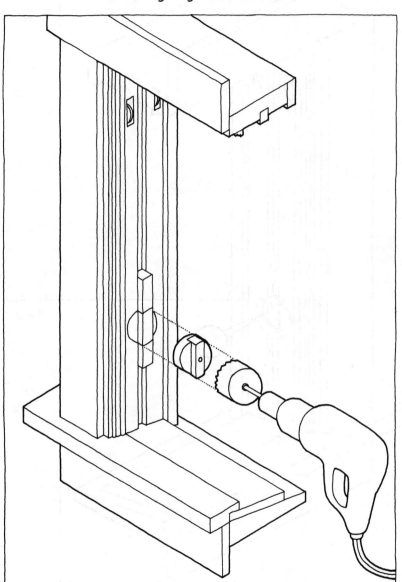

Diagram 27

Double-Hung Windows **39**

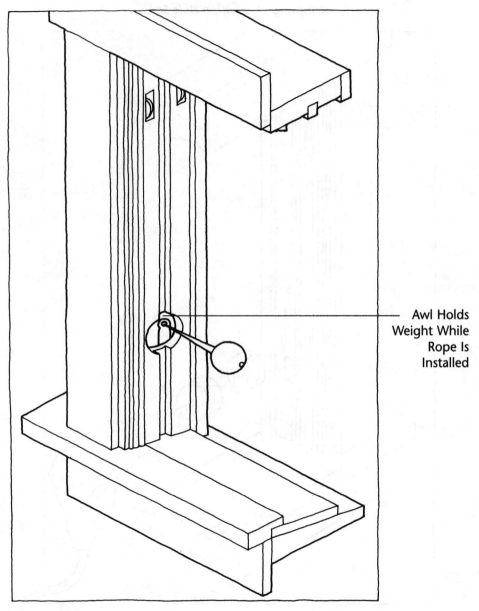

Awl Holds
Weight While
Rope Is
Installed

DIAGRAM 28

to reinstall. Just build up the inner edge with masking tape, apply some wood glue, and reinstall. Keep a small piece of parting bead in its dado so the two broken sections don't start to move. Line it up, let the glue dry, and caulk or otherwise fill the surface gap (Bondo works well here). Take a razor blade to cut away any excess tape. This section will not be removable for future access.

Ultimately, the more room you have for roping the weights the better, so remove the casings whenever possible if you don't have pocket covers.

DUPLEX PULLEYS

Duplex pulleys or sash balances contain spring-wound cables that have small L-brackets at the cables' ends; these brackets attach to the sash. If your cables have snapped or look unreliable, the pulleys should be replaced since the cable cannot be repaired. As I mentioned earlier, these are not a common hardware item and may have to be ordered.

If your pulley is covered with paint, scrape it off or otherwise remove it. The steel casing will have printing on it including a number (like #8 duplex or #10 duplex, etc.) *This is important!* You have to replace it with a like-size pulley. The outer metal casing may be the same dimension, but the inner workings vary according to the size of the sash.

Remove both sash and the parting beads. The cables from the duplex pulleys will be attached to the bottom of each sash via an L-bracket. This is attached with one or two small nails. Pry these out or cut the cables. Note that the section of the parting bead that fits over the pulley has been partially chiseled away to accommodate the pulley (Diagram 29). If you replace the parting bead, you will have to chisel this section away in the new parting bead. You can also run this section against a belt sander and grind it down. The duplex pulley is installed with four nails, two at the top and two at the bottom. Pry it off and install the replacement pulley.

Small windows will often have only one duplex pulley. Larger windows will have one in each side of the jamb.

Reattaching sash to duplex pulleys is much easier with two people doing the work. The cables are tense and are difficult to hold on to while balancing the sash. Mr. Window has done them alone, of course, since he was too cheap to hire any help, but doesn't recommend this

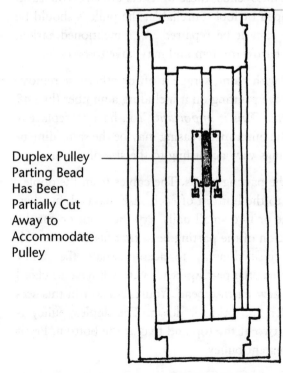

Duplex Pulley
Parting Bead
Has Been
Partially Cut
Away to
Accommodate
Pulley

DIAGRAM 29

approach since it's annoying. Carefully pull the cables from the duplex pulley and nail the brackets to their respective sash. There is no adjustment of the length of the cable. Install the parting beads in the same manner as roped windows, noting the section to be removed in order to fit over the pulley.

After each sash is installed, check for operation. If the sash don't move or close properly, the tension of the pulleys may have to be adjusted. See the directions enclosed with the pulley for this procedure. If you have two different-size sash, you may not be able to obtain perfect tension for both. Be concerned with the upper sash; you can always adjust the stops on the lower if you need to tighten it.

REMOVING INTERLOCKING WEATHER STRIPPING

This is *such* fun. If the material is intact and forms a tight seal, it's worth keeping. If it doesn't line up well with the sash, it's a good idea to replace it. Interlocking weather stripping requires a very precise fit with the sash. Other weather stripping, like spring bronze or vinyl, can be more accommodating, especially if the sash no longer fits well.

Interlocking weather stripping is located on the vertical sides of both upper and lower sash, at the meeting rail, at the sill, and at the top of the jamb where the top rail of the upper sash locks into it. Got that? In other words, it's at all four sides of each sash.

How do you remove it? First, if the lower sash is painted shut, break all of the paint around it, inside and out, and remove the stops. Place a stiff putty knife between the sash and the sill and push upward. Move the sash up and down, spraying lubricant around the edges at the jamb if necessary. If it is stuck closed and you cannot get to the exterior, then place the putty knife between the jamb and the sash and press against the sash, working up and down its height. Also work it between the bottom of the sash and the stool, but only press gently. You're only trying to pop the paint seal. Insert the knife at the meeting rail as well, but only bend the knife slightly. This should loosen the sash enough for you to move it up, if only a few inches. Weather-stripped sash are tougher to loosen up because the interlocking material doesn't allow you to pull the sash forward after the stops are removed.

Push against the top rail (at the corners, not in the middle) and try to force the sash up. Sometimes pounding on the vertical stiles a bit will help to loosen it. Keep working it, up and down, and eventually it will open completely. If it does not move, don't push so hard on the upper rail that you break it loose at the corners! Go back and reinsert the putty knife at all points and continue. Use plenty of lubricant and open the sash as completely as possible.

The lower sash's vertical weather stripping should be held in with two or three nails: one at the top, one at the bottom, and one maybe in the middle. Find the top nail for the right-hand section of weather stripping. This will be very close to the top of the lower sash. Either drive it into the jamb with a nail setter and hammer or insert a small (5-inch or so) pry bar under the weather stripping and pull it out slightly until the head of the nail sticks out enough to grab it with a pair of pliers or wire cutters. Don't worry if you mangle the corner of the weather stripping a bit; it can always be trimmed off with tin snips.

With this nail removed, open the sash and remove the remaining nails. Then lower the sash a bit and move it and the weather stripping in toward you. You may need to put a putty knife under the weather stripping to ease it out. Place the weather stripping aside. The ropes will probably be nailed to the side of the sash. Cut these and knot the ends, easing them toward the pulleys. Set the sash aside. Remove the other piece of weather stripping. If you find a cardboard shim (thin pieces of cardboard) under either or both pieces, save it; you will need it during reassembly.

Remove the parting beads *carefully*. The lower ends of the weather stripping at the upper sash are held fast with two nails. Only one section of material has to be removed in order to remove the sash. Typically, as with the lower, the right side was the last to be installed, so remove it, although it doesn't make a lot of difference. Well, okay, if you're a member of a radical left-handed advocacy group it probably makes a *huge* difference.

The upper sash will have to move to allow you to remove all of the nails holding the weather stripping. Break all of the paint seal inside and out. *Don't get too aggressive!* Why not? Because when the side of the sash is routed to receive the weather stripping, the edge that slides against the parting bead is no longer the complete thickness of the sash. It's thinner and can be split if the sash has been sealed shut with paint and you break it free with too much force. This is true when the parting beads are removed as well. If it does split, you'll have to repair it with glue and small wire nails. Insert a stiff putty knife between the top of the sash and the jamb on the exterior side and try to force the sash down. After it moves an inch or so, force it back up and then down again. Continue to do this until it moves more or less freely. Usually, it has so much paint on it that it will move only quite stiffly. Scrape the paint from the jamb and spray it with lubricant to ease your work. You can also take a heat gun or torch and strip the paint from the jamb if it's really built up.

If the sash moves beyond the bottom of the weather stripping and will clear it, then you will not have to remove any of the weather stripping.

Once you have it moving, close it and remove the lower two nails of the right-side weather stripping. Lower the sash and remove the upper nail(s), which will be near the pulley. Move both sash and weather stripping down toward the sill, moving the material down and around the pulley. Remove it and the sash from the jamb and install your new ropes.

REINSTALLATION

This is more fun. Adjust and install the ropes for the upper sash. You may have noticed that the old ropes were nailed at the sash instead of knotted. The thinking was to avoid having the knot jam up against the weather stripping. I have usually been able to avoid this by forcing the knot deep into the knot hole and securing it with a nail. If the hole is too shallow or the groove for the weather stripping cut too close to the hole, then nail the rope in three or four places with nails similar to the ones you removed (wire nails with small heads). There will be no knot at the end. Be sure to test the length of the ropes before installing the weather stripping.

There are copper nails made specifically for weather stripping, but they aren't available at all hardware stores. You might find them at a marine boating shop. Their heads will not corrode like those of steel nails if they get exposed to moisture. Usually, it only happens with the nail or nails near the bottom of the weather stripping at the lower sash. They can also corrode at the meeting rail if too much water drips down on them from window washing.

Place the section of weather stripping you removed into the groove on the side of the sash. Sometimes it helps to run a file through this groove to clean it out, or use a folded piece of 50-D or similar-grade sandpaper. Insert the left side of the sash against the weather stripping still nailed at the jamb and move the right side against its section of the jamb. Lower the sash, and push the weather stripping up and around the pulley, nailing it there. Raise the sash and nail at the bottom. Nail near the pulley and install the parting beads as usual.

Note: Sometimes, with interlocking weather stripping, the lower half of the parting bead has a narrow channel cut into it to receive the edge of the weather stripping. Look closely at the old parting bead for signs of this. You can duplicate this channel by cutting into the parting bead with a handsaw or running the edge of a sharp chisel into it after the parting bead is installed. Or you can cut along the edge of the weather stripping with metal snips, removing ⅛ inch or so and running the edge on a belt sander or filing it. The resulting edge will not be as smooth as the factory-finished one. You must do one or the other for the sash to line up correctly. If you decide to snip off the edge of the weather stripping, then line it up with its old nail holes to be sure it's back where it belongs.

Nail one side of the lower weather stripping to the jamb; attach the ropes to the sash. Be sure the bottom end of the vertical piece locks into the piece attached to the sill. If the sash were locked together properly when you began the disassembly, then, again, use the old nail holes as guides to realign the weather stripping. Install the other piece of material and the sash in the same manner as the upper sash. If you cannot insert a nail in the existing nail hole when installing the second piece of weather stripping, then prepunch a small hole and nail there. You'll probably need to hold the nail with a needlenose pliers and toenail (hammer at an angle) it in, setting it with a nail set.

Be sure the section of weather stripping at the meeting rail, where the sash lock together, is clean and free of dirt and paint. It can be cleaned by scraping it with a small file or a screwdriver. If, after cleaning, the two sash do not lock together, it may be necessary to take a wide putty knife and spread the material slightly so the two pieces slip together.

Close the window and look out and up through the lower sash at this section of weather stripping. You should be able to see if each piece is clearing the other properly. If not, gradually spread the material out with the putty knife (it may even be spread too wide, in which case you will have to tap it back to a narrower profile; you can do this by placing a small file against the weather stripping and tapping it with a hammer). Check also that the vertical weather stripping is aligned properly so the sash are close enough to lock.

There are various pulley- and weight-replacement systems available as alternatives. Quaker Hardware is probably the best known. It is a track system that is installed after the pulleys and parting beads are removed. In their place, a metal track with a spring metal parting bead (the tension of which holds the sash in place) is installed, holding the sash. I haven't found them to be as good as the results from repairing the old system. Marvin makes a system as well that is even more difficult to install than the Quaker system. In a sense, pulleys and weights are primitive, but they always work and can always be repaired. If a track replacement system breaks or the tension gives out, good luck repairing it.

CHAPTER TWO

CASEMENT WINDOWS, AWNING WINDOWS

CASEMENT WINDOWS

Casement windows open out like doors and, as a rule, have one of two types of hinges: butt hinges (found on most doors) or friction hinges. Butt hinges are visible on the exterior of the sash and require an opener (an adjustable "arm") to control how far the sash will open and keep wind from slamming it around. The friction hinges are self-locking and are routed into the top and bottom rails of the sash.

Casement with Butt Hinges

Casement with Friction Hinges

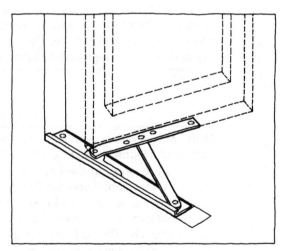

DIAGRAM 31

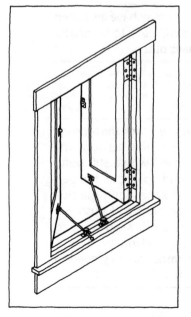

DIAGRAM 30

You may have operable casements and not realize it if they have been painted and caulked shut and the hardware removed. Or the original casements may have deteriorated and fixed sash been installed in their place. The easiest clue if all the hardware is gone (and you don't have butt hinges) is any sign of an old lock. If removed, the screw holes would be filled. The locks were almost always located at the center of one of the vertical stiles. Look carefully for a depression from the lock. If you suspect there was a lock, scrape the stile and look for either two or four holes filled with spackle. To its side, on the jamb, will be a depression. This is the former location of the lock strike and will also be filled.

Which side will the lock be on? Typically, if the windows were installed symmetrically, that is, side by side, the sash to your left (looking from the inside) will open right to left; the window on your right will open left to right. If a single window, I would say opening left to right is more common.

Beware: If the window has been sealed shut, it may have also been nailed shut from the outside. This means it will have to be gradually opened from the inside to force the nails out.

Okay, Mr. Window, just how do you open a stuck-shut-forever casement window? Good question. Break the paint between the sash and the jamb (at the point where it closes) with a stiff putty knife or a heat gun. If you can break the outside paint, all the better. In either case, after it's broken, force the knife along the side at the bottom corner (away from the hinge side) and push out more forcefully. The sash should spring out a bit. Keep working the knife up the length of the sash, gradually working it outward. Do the same at the top and bottom of the sash. You may need to push at two different points at the same time.

These can really be stuck, like they're squeezed into an opening too small for their size. Push out gradually so you don't break the sash or glass, or loosen the bottom rail. If you have friction hinges, they can really be stuck, so work them back and forth gradually, spraying with lubricant. If you force the sash open too abruptly and the hinge is frozen, you can stress the joints too much.

Look out for rusted hinges, loose glass, and loose bottom rails. Sometimes these rails are so loose that they will fall off as the window is opened. If this is the case with your casements, hold on to the rails until the sash is removed and repaired.

Okay, so now you've gotten the window open. Now try to close it! It may not close. See Chapter 4 for everything you always wanted to know about casement window repair but, with three college degrees, never thought you'd have to ask.

Your casement will, as noted, have either butt hinges or friction hinges. Butt hinges are almost always salvageable. Friction hinges, mostly the ones attached to the lower rails, can be rusted beyond repair. To remove butt hinges, unscrew them at the jamb. If the screw slots are filled with paint, use your screwdriver like a chisel (a highly recommended practice for ruining screwdrivers, by the way, so use a cheap one) and tap it with a hammer until the paint is chipped out. Note the presence of any shims under the hinges on the jamb side. *These are important!* If these are not replaced, the sash will not close properly. I often leave them attached loosely to the jamb with the hinge screws so I'll know to reinstall them.

If you have friction hinges, unscrew them at the header (upper jamb) and at the sill. If the screws will turn but can't be removed (usually at the lower hinge), loosen them completely and slip a tool, such as a small pry bar or stiff putty knife, under the hinge and pry up slightly. Let the hinge return to the sill and the screw head should be sticking out enough to grab the head with a pliers or small pry bar. Remove the screws and then loosen the top hinge.

Gradually ease the sash away from the jamb. You may have to slip a stiff putty knife under the hinges to force them out of the jamb. With the sash removed, spray the hinges with more lubricant or penetrating oil and work them back and forth. If they're really stuck, take a propane torch to them.

Note: These hinges can have shims under them as well, particularly on the bottom hinge.

Your casement may be weather-stripped with either spring bronze material or interlocking weather stripping. Interlocking weather stripping on a casement window consists of a piece routed into the sash on three sides, with opposing pieces nailed to the jamb. One piece locks into the other. On the hinge side (butt hinges or, if you have friction hinges, where butt hinges would otherwise be located), a channel is cut that fits into a corresponding piece of weather stripping on the jamb.

Like double-hung windows with interlocking material, casements require a precise fit of sash and weather stripping in order to close and lock properly. It can often be reused or portions of it replaced with spring bronze. Please see Chapter 4 for details.

AWNING WINDOWS/HOPPER VENT

An awning window is similar to a casement except it opens horizontally rather than vertically; that is, take a casement, turn it on its side, and open it. *Voilà,* an awning window.

Awning windows will have either butt hinges or friction hinges. If the butt hinges are on the bottom rail, the sash will either drop in or drop out. If it drops in, it's called a hopper vent or a hopper light. Sometimes a small chain is attached to the jamb and the sash to control how far the sash will travel (in either direction). If the hinges are on the top, the sash will most likely open in and need to be held open with an opener or even a piece of wood.

If friction hinges are used, they will be on the stiles. With either hinge, a lock will be present at either the top or bottom rail, depending on how the sash opens.

Simple awning windows are often found in basements for basic ventilation. Sometimes awning windows or hopper vents were installed over very tall double-hung windows.

Awning windows open and are repaired in the same manner as casement windows, and are fairly easy to work on.

CHAPTER THREE

FIXED WINDOWS

No, a fixed window does not imply a surgical procedure has been performed for the purpose of birth control. "Fixed" simply means the window does not open. A single sash can be fixed or a double-hung window without pulleys can be considered fixed. As these are inoperable, there is little reason to remove them or do any repairs other than reglazing and repainting.

But . . . you may have some problems, such as deteriorated wood sections or a whole sash that is pulling away from its opening. Also, the glass may be quite loose or pulling away. You may want to remove the sash in order to completely sand and repaint it.

FIXED SINGLE SASH

A fixed single sash is either installed from the outside of the opening or from the inside. If installed from the inside, the sash will have stops like a double-hung window. It will rest against a parting bead or similar stop on the exterior. Typically, at the time of installation, the sash would be held against the bead or stop and secured with a small number of finish nails toenailed into the jamb.

To remove the sash, loosen the paint around the stops and gently pry them off. You'll have to find the space between the edge of the stop and the casing, and insert a stiff putty knife and gradually ease it out. With all three stops removed, hammer a couple of large nails about halfway down the jamb where the stops were removed. Only insert them part of the way in and an inch away from the sash. Why? So they'll act as stops when the sash starts falling in as you pry it loose.

Insert a stiff putty knife between the outside edge of the sash and the parting bead or stop it is pressed against. If your fixed window is too high up to comfortably reach from a ladder and if it has opening side windows, you *can* break various OSHA (Occupational Safety and Health Administration) safety regulations by hanging out these side windows and doing your work with the putty knife. It's a bit of a reach, but can be done (not that Mr. Window, now on a permanent sabbatical, would ever consider doing this, either). Break the paint all around and force the sash inward.

If there aren't any nails holding it in, lucky you! Push it in until it hits the nails you put in as stops. While holding the sash, remove your nails and work it back and forth until it lifts out. If the sash has been nailed in place, locate the nails by running a putty knife between the sash and the jamb. You can then attempt to cut them with a hacksaw blade or drive the putty knife into them with a hammer and break them off. Proceed with removing the sash.

If your fixed sash was installed from the outside, you most likely won't have interior stops. The sash will be nailed against the jamb from the exterior side and then caulked or otherwise sealed around its edge. To remove it, break the paint on both sides with a hammer and stiff putty knife. From the inside, force the knife between the sash and the jamb, and slowly push it out.

Obviously, it helps to have a second person outside, but it can be done alone, even if from a second story or higher. To do so, you will have to keep it from falling all the way out. You can screw a piece of chain to the top rail and then to the jamb. If it's a large sash, you should really have two people. There are some methodologies that even Mr. Window frowns upon. The sash shouldn't move very fast, since it's been painted shut and the paint buildup acts as a brake.

As the sash loosens and falls outward, move it back and forth to loosen it and lift it up and out.

CHAPTER FOUR

REPAIRS, WEATHER STRIPPING, REPAINTING, REFINISHING, REDEMPTION

All right, redemption may be pushing things a bit. However, it is possible to repair even the most deteriorated window. You'll have to decide whether it's worth keeping or replacing. The criteria usually involve:

✓ Time and money
✓ Historical or architectural accuracy
✓ The challenge of doing the work
✓ Time and money, again

If you have more time than money, then by all means repair. If you have sufficient money to replace, then you have the option to do that or repair. If you have tons of money, move to Paris or Tahiti and forget about your windows.

Replacement windows come in generic styles and kits as well as exact duplicates of your existing windows, these latter ones being the most expensive. The problem with using generic replacements for your worst windows is that they won't match the old ones. You may feel compelled to replace everything, which can be costly.

Local building and energy codes vary. If you replace all your windows, you may have to replace them with insulated windows (existing old windows are single-glaze—that is, they have one piece of glass; insulated windows have two or even three panes of glass with an insulating space between panes). If you replace individual windows or sash, single-glaze will better match your existing windows.

If you replace a single sash of a double-hung window with a new, matching sash with insulated glass, the sash will be too heavy for the weights and you will have to adjust them accordingly. Also, the bulk of energy savings from insulated windows does not come from the glass, but rather the jamb, with its factory weather stripping and seal. Simply adding insulated sash to your old double-hung jambs will improve your heat bill, but not as significantly as whole new windows will. If you're thinking along these lines, I suggest replacing the entire window.

Also, attempting to replace single-glaze glass in an existing operable sash with insulated glass simply does not pay off unless you've got *lots* of time on your hands. Most residential-size sash, which are normally 1⅜ inches thick, will not easily accommodate the added thickness of insulated glass. In fact, you may have to rout away so much wood that you weaken the sash.

Okay, so you've decided to repair your existing windows. If they are painted shut, broken, inoperable, leaky, and rattling, they can be greatly improved; but *they will not be new windows!* They will be quite serviceable, though, and offer a long life. Look at it this way: If your house is eighty years old and has the original windows, which have survived years of indifference, don't you think that after they're repaired they'll be good for a few more decades?

THE HAWAII FACTOR

Very important: If it's going to cost you, say, $10,000 or more to replace all of your windows with matching, historically accurate windows (in after-tax dollars), how much heat will you have to save (and over how many years) to make up for all the heat and sun you could have been soaking up on Maui if you'd spent the money (and any interest on it) by flying off in the dead of winter to sunny paradise? And how many trips would you be able to take? Life's short, so consider your priorities.

REPAIR PROBLEMS

The most common problems with old wood windows are:

- ✓ Excessive paint buildup
- ✓ Broken ropes
- ✓ Broken glass or loose glazing compound (the stuff that holds the glass in; sometimes called putty)
- ✓ Loose corners
- ✓ Rotted or deteriorated wood
- ✓ Missing or broken hardware
- ✓ Sloppy or tight fit

Paint Buildup

This one's easy. You can figure that a residence gets painted every eight to ten years on the exterior. Interiors will vary, but kitchens and bathrooms are typically repainted more often than other rooms. So, if your house is seventy years old, you've got, technically speaking, *lots o' paint*. Eventually you reach what a coatings (paint) chemist would call critical thickness; that is, the surface has too much paint and cannot guarantee intercoat adhesion (new paint won't stick well). The more you build up the paint, especially on the exterior, the more often you'll have to paint because the paint will fail and begin to lift off, particularly on the weathered sides.

Old paint can be removed by various methods, including heat (torch, heat gun, heat plate), chemicals (various removers, liquid and paste), scraping, and sanding (belt sanders, finish sanders, disk sanders).

All these methods have their strong and weak points. I'll take them one at a time. I'll preface my comments with forewarnings about lead-based paint and other such evils.

Lead!

Current and proposed legislation addresses the removal and disposal of lead-based paint. Some paint stores sell testing kits to determine the presence of lead in paint, water, soil, etc. I do not propose to explain legalities here. Think again if you believe Mr. Window will provide guidelines that could later be used against him in court. If it is a concern of yours, then I suggest you contact your local EPA (Environmental Protection Agency) office or public health department regarding local and national laws. I guarantee it will be an interesting exercise in obfuscation.

Basically, the guidelines call for the paint to be removed with the least-disruptive method possible and disposed of in a prescribed manner. The regulations may vary depending on the amount of contaminate and whether you're a homeowner doing your own work. If a contractor removes lead-based paint on your property in an improper manner and the neighbors let fly with a lawsuit, you, too, could be on the receiving end. If you're going to remove the paint yourself, I would suggest that you do the work in an empty garage (for loose sash and trim) in which you can contain the contaminated dust and refuse and can later clean and decontaminate your work area, following acceptable guidelines.

Justified or not, lead paint has become the asbestos of the 1990s.

For further information, *Old House Journal* has reprints of their July-August 1992 article entitled "Getting Rid of Lead," available by calling 1-800-356-9313.

Safety Considerations
Be forewarned this type of repair work will expose you to a variety of fumes, dusts, odors, noises, and solvents. The world of chemistry may be wonderful, but a few precautions are in order.

Wear some basic safety equipment! This includes respirators (for smoke and fumes), heavy dust masks (for sanding dust), safety glasses, heavy gloves, and ear protectors.

There are various manufacturers of respirators, including Wilson, North, and 3M. Safety equipment suppliers, listed in the Yellow Pages, are a good source. Explain the type of work you will be doing in order to get the appropriate filters. Some filters are only good for organic vapors (solvents, chemical paint removers), some for fine particulates (smoke, dust), and some for dust alone. 3M offers an excellent heavy dust mask (not the thin paper mask, good for light dust only), which is an industry standard (General Dust and Sanding Respirator, #8710). Buy a box of them (they run about ninety cents per mask). Their effectiveness, like any other respirator or mask, will depend on the environment in which you are working (enclosed, outdoors, the material being sanded, the parts of particulate per million, etc.) and the fit (for example, they are not nearly as effective for people with beards). If you're indoors and dealing with excessive dust, you may want a mask to filter out the very fine particles. If so, purchase a half-face respirator with HEPA filters. Your supplier can give you complete information.

Use heavy gloves if you're going to be using paint remover or other solvents. Elbow-length gloves will provide the most protection, especially if you're working on overhead woodwork.

There are three types of ear protectors available with which I am familiar: earmuff-style protectors, disposable foam, and a semipermanent hard plastic insert. I like to combine the disposable foam pieces (about forty cents a pair; they are actually reusable indefinitely and are washable) and the earmuff piece. Either one is okay alone and meets standards for small power tools, but together they seem to filter out more noise.

Heat Removal
Heat removal is quiet, fairly quick, and produces solid chunks of paint refuse for easy cleanup. This method works best against many layers of paint (the more the better). The heat softens the paint so it can be scraped off to bare wood. The drawback is the smoke, so wear a respirator with appropriate filters. If you heat lead-based paint, you can vaporize the lead and it can spread beyond the worksite. Read the industry guidelines when using this or any other paint-removal method.

Small propane torches work rapidly, but are a bit difficult to control and may leave torch marks, although these usually sand out. If you use one of these to remove paint from woodwork or siding, there is the problem of an open flame. For house stripping, you may need a permit from the local fire marshal. Keep a hose or container of water nearby. Electric paint removers have a heating element similar to a burner on an electric stove, but are rectangular in shape. These tools work quickly, too, although not as fast as torches, and are easier to control. Again, they work best with many layers of paint.

Heat guns are the slowest of the three tools, but the easiest to control and particularly good for intricate work. All three should be held against the painted surface until the paint is soft enough to scrape off. Usually, the paint will begin to smoke; sometimes a small flame will erupt. Just scrape it off and blow the flame out. The paint will cool and harden in about twenty seconds or so.

The temperatures of different heat guns and plates vary. Some are considered to be less deleterious when removing lead-based paint than others. Again, refer to the published guidelines.

Keep the heat away from the glass! Now that the statute of limitations has passed, Mr. Window is willing to admit he did not always follow this caveat and has cracked some glass on occasion. Just strip the flat areas of the stiles and rails.

After cleaning the paint off with heat, some sanding or cleaning by solvent may be necessary to remove the residue and bits of finish you could not scrape away. The key is to let the heat do the work and scrape it as clean as possible. Make a second sweep with the heat if too much old paint remains. After some practice, you should be able to scrape almost all of the finish off and get down to bare wood.

Chemical Removal

Paint remover is the most expensive way to go. Most standard removers will require at least two applications or more to clean the paint away. There is little reason to use them except for varnish or shellac removal, or for removing paint near the glass. The standard methylene chloride removers are more effective, in my opinion, than the water-rinsable removers. They are also more toxic and require solvent, preferably lacquer thinner, for a final cleaning and rinsing of the wood.

Another type of chemical remover is made by Dumond Chemicals, Inc. Peel Away paint remover consists of an alkaline paste and a specially treated paper that covers the remover after it has been applied to a painted surface. The paper prevents Peel Away from drying out and allows it to continuously work away at the paint. Twenty-four hours or so later, as the paper is removed, it pulls the remover and paint with it. It works quite well, but it's a tedious process. There are also some other similar products on the market. Peel Away comes with a limited amount of treated paper, and extra sections of it are expensive. I've found that for narrow areas like window sash stiles and rails, wide duct tape can easily and inexpensively take the place of the paper.

Standard chemical removers are thickly applied to painted or varnished surfaces and then removed with scrapers or putty knives after the paint or varnish has softened. Sometimes an almost immediate second application is required over the first if it begins to dry too quickly. Additional applications may be required to remove all of the finish. A final rinse with lacquer thinner will remove any remaining residue.

Warning! All chemical removers are toxic, skinophobic solutions. Wear a respirator, eye protection, and heavy elbow-length gloves. I would also suggest wearing an old sweatshirt because the solution is bound to spatter in your direction. And no wearing Bermuda shorts, either!

Along these lines, you may want to consider tank dipping. Generally speaking, there are two types of dipping operations: cold tanks and hot tanks. A cold dipping immerses the items to be stripped in a large quantity of chemical stripper, similar to what you would purchase in a gallon can. After sufficient time for the chemicals to dissolve the old finish, the item is rinsed and neutralized, preferably with lacquer thinner rather than water, as the latter can raise the grain of wood items. A hot tank uses a caustic material, similar to lye, dissolved in a tank of heated water. This process tends to discolor wood, raise its grain, and loosen joints to varying degrees, depending on the operator and system. The fees for hot tanks are typically lower than those for cold tanks. Cold tanks can also raise the wood grain if they rinse with water.

A tank operation is responsible for toxic waste disposal and eliminates your exposure to dust and fumes. The drawback, of course, is the cost. If you are considering this route, have a sample done first, perhaps a piece of woodwork, so you can determine if the results and fees are acceptable. If you're dipping window sash, the operator will probably not guarantee against glass breakage.

Scraping

Scrapers, if kept very sharp, can cut through many layers of paint, but the process is haphazard. Dependence solely on scrapers usually results in gouging the wood. If the paint is really flaky and loose, you'll have a better degree of success. Also, if the paint was applied over varnish, it can scrape off more easily. Otherwise, progress is a wonderful thing, so consider using heat or sanders.

That said, I wholeheartedly recommend Red Devil's carbide paint scraper. It's expensive, but it does wonders, especially on varnish. Unlike most paint scrapers, this one offers a high degree of control when cutting through finishes. It isn't commonly available and will probably have to be ordered from your Red Devil dealer.

Sanding

The advantage of sanding is that you have some control over how much paint is removed. You may only need to spot-sand rough areas, whereas with heat or chemicals you have less control over the degree of removal.

A disk sander is the fastest sanding tool, but it also throws dust everywhere.

A belt sander with a dust bag attached is a better alternative if you're trying to control dust. Although there will still be dust that the bag doesn't catch, it's in a more confined area. Very fine dust, however, can be carried some distance away from the worksite. Makita makes wonderful, affordable sanders, particularly their finish sander.

Use a coarse paper for extensive paint removal (like 24 or 36 grit). Follow up with a finish sander to remove the marks left by the sanding belt or disk. Use a 50-grit finish paper followed by 100-grit. Sand until you're satisfied with the smoothness of the wood. A smoother finish can be gotten from using higher-grit papers (150, 220, etc.).

Figure you'll go through one sanding belt per window (two sash) and two to three pieces of finish paper (four pieces to a sheet). If you have a lot of sanding to do (say, exterior work, a floor, or a lot of sash), buy the sandpaper by the sleeve and the belts by the box. Paint stores will give you a discount for bulk purchases.

Some manufacturers are producing disk sanders with shrouds and vacuum attachments. American-International Tool Ind., Inc. (1116-B Park Ave., Cranston, RI 02910; 1-401-942-7855), offers an S344 Sander Vac 5-inch disk sander with dust collector that, according to their literature, meets Massachusetts lead-abatement standards. This and other such tools are well worth considering. Bear in mind that the dust collection is effective only if the entire area of the disk is engaged. On a sash rail, for instance, you would have to place a board next to it so the disk and its shroud never have open space under them for the dust to escape. FEIN Power Tools, Inc. (1-800-441-9878), offers a sander and vacuum combination that does not depend on full contact because the dust is sucked up through the disk itself. It's a very cool-looking arrangement. Call them for a brochure and current price.

Bosch also makes a series of disk sanders similar to FEIN's, but without the accompanying vacuum. They have small collection bags that attach to the sanders, but you can attach a vacuum hose instead. Use a shop vac and put some water in the canister. When the dust passes into it, the water should prevent much of the fine dust debris from blowing out the exhaust.

Once the paint or other finish is removed, the sash can be prefinished before reinstalling them. The jamb and casings can also be painted. This is a much simpler way of painting than with the window assembled.

Regardless of which method you choose, be aware of the dispersal and disposal of lead and other paint debris. With that and the preceding statements, I have not only done my duty as an author to provide critical information, but also made it generic enough that it can be interpreted about a dozen different ways. Who said a how-to-do-it book can't be creative?

Although rope replacement has already been covered, it's worth emphasizing replacement if the existing ropes look okay, but you're going to disassemble the window anyway. Number 8 synthetic-cotton mix sash rope is recommended. If your local hardware store does not carry it, try a rope wholesaler. If you only need a bundle or two and they will not sell less than a case, ask for the names of their retail customers, from whom you may be able to make a smaller purchase. Unless an anti-window terrorist attacks your house and cuts this rope, it will last indefinitely.

Broken Ropes

The ropes originally used in double-hung windows were made from cotton, which has limited durability. When was the last time you saw a sixty-year-old T-shirt that was intact and usable? Add to that the amount of paint buildup over the years and you can expect these ropes to start breaking. You can still buy 100 percent cotton sash rope, but I don't recommend it. A better product is a mix of cotton and synthetic material that maintains the appearance of traditional cotton rope, moves smoothly through a pulley, and has greater strength and toughness. These ropes will last indefinitely. Sash chain is an alternative, but it's very costly and unnecessary for most residential sash. Sash rope comes in different thicknesses, which correlate to their numbers (#7 sash rope, #8 sash rope, etc.). I recommend only #8 sash rope for all but the largest windows. Although #8 rope will usually be sufficient for these windows, you may want to use #10 sash rope as a precaution.

Rope is a low-cost item in window repair, so don't skimp on the size or because of price. For more information on rope replacement, please see pages 16–26.

Broken Glass

I rarely replace a piece of broken glass. That's why there are glaziers in the world. In fact, it would upset the natural balance of life if glaziers didn't replace broken glass. You have four general options for replacing broken glass:

✓ Do it all yourself.
✓ Call a glazier to do the work on site.
✓ Take the sash to a glazier or a hardware store that does glass replacement.
✓ Remove all the broken glass and old putty yourself and then call a glazier or take the sash out for glass installation.

Keep in mind that, like lead-based paint, glazing can be a source of hazards, including lead and a minor amount of asbestos, which was used as a binder in some products. If this is a concern to you and you still wish to remove it, keep a spray bottle of water nearby and keep wetting the glazing as you chip it off. Again, refer to any published guidelines.

Replacing the Glass Yourself

Well, it will be a learning experience. *All* the old putty has to be removed either by hacking it out with a chisel and hammer or by softening the putty with a heat gun or torch and scraping it out. Using heat is a cleaner approach, but it will bubble the paint near the glazing. With the putty removed, take off the small glazing points that secure the glass to the sash. Carefully remove the glass and scrape out the putty underneath it.

Measure for the new piece of glass. Keep in mind that the sash may no longer be square, so you should measure in several places. If it's a lower sash, it may have a check rail. This is a dado cut into the underside of the upper rail into which the glass slides. You'll have to allow for this distance when measuring. The glass can also be measured from inside the sash. Most older residential glass is single strength in thickness. It is worth replacing with double-strength (DS) glass at a low additional cost. This should not adversely affect the sash and weight balance. If your windows seem particularly heavy and your house or building has more elegant origins, you may have ¼-inch-thick glass. You must replace it with the same thickness of glass if you expect the sash and weights to work properly. If you are uncertain about the thickness, take a small piece of the glass to be replaced to your glass supplier.

Glass can be purchased from a glass company or a hardware store, the latter often being the more expensive of the two sources. Take your measurements and purchase the glass, carefully transporting it standing on edge, *not lying flat,* unless you like buying more glass after your first batch has cracked.

You'll need some glazing compound or putty. DAP is a common brand and it works fairly well. Assuming that you have other windows with missing glazing compound, buy a quart of the stuff. Empty the contents of the can and knead it thoroughly. My experience with DAP is it tends to be soft and oily at the top of the can, and drier at the bottom. Kneading produces a more consistent material. Heating the compound a bit (place the can in a container of hot water or heat briefly with a heat gun) will also soften it. You'll also need some push-in glazing points.

Warning! Some products advertised as glazing are more like spackle and terrible to work with. DAP always works if you have any doubts about another product.

Place a small bead of latex caulking against the edge of the sash where the glass will rest. Install the glass and press against the caulk. If the glass springs back a bit at any point, the sash is probably warped, so don't get too aggressive with the glass. You can also bed the glass in a thin line of glazing compound pressed smoothly and uniformly against the sash. Insert the glazing points about every 12 inches or so. Glazing points are important because they hold the glass in place. The glazing compound only seals the glass against water and wind. When in doubt, use a few extra points.

Take a handful of glazing compound and knead again until soft. Press it against the edge of the glass and, if you have a check rail, into that as well. It is easier to smooth out the compound with a glazing knife. You can use a stiff putty knife or even a narrow chisel. The glazing knife and putty knives are available at paint stores, glass shops, and hardware stores. Just be sure the edge is very clean (rub some sandpaper on it if necessary) so it does not drag the putty off the glass. Get the glazing compound as smooth as you can. Ideally, you should be able to look through the glass from the inside and not see any glazing compound. The compound should have a narrow-enough profile that it can be painted with just a slight bead of paint running onto the glass in order to seal the edge. None of this should be visible when looking out through the window. Of course, ideals are great. Chances are the glazing compound and paint lines on your old windows have crept over onto the glass over the years, so you need not feel compelled to be a perfectionist.

Different brands of glazing compound have different curing times. If uncertain, allow a week before painting. A common error is to leave it unpainted after replacing glass. Eventually, the compound will dry and fall out and lose its effectiveness as a seal. Then you get to repeat this process all over again. You can paint it the same day, but this isn't the best approach because it takes much longer to dry and harden.

Note: You can paint it before the glazing compound has completely cured only if you use an oil-based primer! This is *really* important. If you apply latex products over fresh glazing compound, the solvents from the compound will try to pass through the latex and cause both materials to crack. If this happens, the glazing compound will have to be applied again. Oil-based products will form a film that does not allow the drying solvents from the glazing compound to escape in such a way as to cause any cracks.

The main drawback to do-it-yourself replacement is the glass cracking as you install or being the wrong size because your measurement was too optimistic and now the glass won't fit your slightly out-of-square sash. That's why I like glaziers.

On-Site Glaziers

Not cheap! Probably thirty-five to forty dollars per hour depending on where you live, plus the cost of the glass (sold by the square foot). Any work done off a ladder, that is, without removing the sash, will be the most expensive as it is the most time-consuming. Still, the work is guaranteed and any glass breakage is the glazier's problem.

Taking the Sash to a Glazier or Hardware Store

Sometimes the shop rate may be cheaper than the on-site rate. Hardware stores are convenient, but it depends on who's doing the work, since they will charge by the hour and some individuals may be slower than others. A glass shop may be faster and less expensive for the glass.

Hack Out the Old Putty Yourself and Have Others Install the Glass

This is the best of all worlds if you have budget considerations. Glaziers usually aren't that fond of chiseling out old putty. Many glaziers work primarily on new windows that use special caulking and metal stops to secure the glass. They may have little experience with older windows. Even with an experienced worker, the bulk of their labor fee comes from cleaning out the old glass and putty. So, if you do the grunt work and provide the glazier with clean sash ready for glass, you'll keep your cost down and leave the more fragile work to others. You may even want to do your own finish-glazing and just have the glazier cut and install the glass with points. This, too, is a cost saver.

Missing or Loose Glazing Compound

If the exterior paint is in poor condition, then the glazing compound usually needs some work as well. When removing deteriorated material, don't get too aggressive. If it's cracked yet tight, leave it. Otherwise, you're likely to crack the glass and then you'll get to remove all of the compound. Reglaze with new putty and rub some into the cracks and gaps of the old-but-intact glazing. Allow to cure and then paint.

Note: If you're going to sand or otherwise remove the exterior paint, do so before replacing glass or glazing compound. Otherwise, the compound gets full of dust and dirt from your work and it's just generally messy-looking. Also, let the compound cure for a week or so before washing the glass. If you wash prematurely, water can get behind the glazing compound and loosen it or otherwise affect its seal.

Loose Corners

Older wood sash are assembled with mortise-and-tenon corners held in place with two pins or thick nails per corner as shown below.

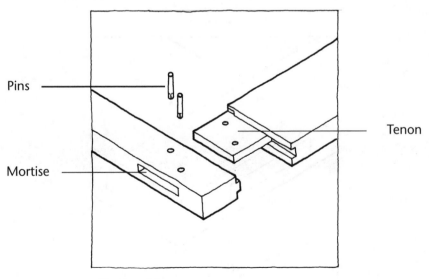

Pins

Tenon

Mortise

DIAGRAM 32

As the paint deteriorates, the pins become exposed to moisture and can rust and loosen. The lower rails ultimately loosen and can even fall out. If the rails soak up enough water they can rot away, especially at the corners. Don't worry, you can fix them. Really.

Note: If the rail has dropped and the glass has been reglazed since the drop, you will not be able to push the rail all the way up into its correct position unless the old glass is moved up first. This requires removing all of the glazing compound and, with the sash upside down, gently pushing the glass back where it belongs. If it is a new piece of glass, installed to the now new dimension of the dropped rail, you can't do anything unless you replace the glass.

Assuming that the rail is simply loose and wobbly, turn the sash on its side so you're looking at the end of the tenon. Drill two holes, at a diagonal, on either side of the tenon. Then either drive a 16-penny (16d) galvanized finish nail into each hole or use a deck screw (be sure to countersink the head). Repeat on the other side as shown below.

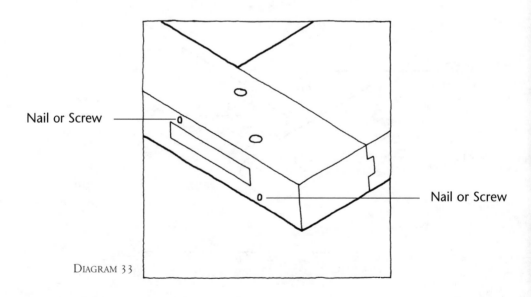

Nail or Screw

Nail or Screw

DIAGRAM 33

If the area has weathered, apply some waterproof automotive body filler or epoxy over it and sand flush when dry (see "Fillers," page 75).

Rotted or Deteriorated Wood

Let's make a distinction between weathered wood and wood rot. If wood is kept sealed with paint or similar material and this seal is consistently maintained, then, in theory, the wood should never deteriorate due to moisture or weather problems. Why? Because Mr. Window says so, that's why. Aside from that, when wood "weathers," it absorbs moisture and expands; it then shrinks as it dries. As the process continues, the wood begins to disassemble, in a sense: The surface gets rough or splintery, cracks develop, warpage sets in, etc. Moisture penetrates wood if it isn't sealed with paint or like material. So, if the paint on a window is flaking or even nonexistent, then the sash will begin to weather and split and all those fun things. True rot is another issue.

Rot is the result of waterborne organisms that like to eat wood until it's all soft and powdery and "punky." If you can easily drive a tool, such as a screwdriver, through a section of your sash (almost always the bottom rail and the lower few inches of the two stiles) and the wood disintegrates before you, then you are the lucky winner of a rotted sash. Either problem can be repaired thanks once again to the wonderful world of chemistry.

Let's start with a weathered sash with a bad bottom rail, one with missing or badly deteriorated tenons. This can be any kind of sash; the repairs are all the same.

Turn the sash on its side and dig out all of the bad tenon. If it's wet, dry it out with a heat gun or hair dryer. If you suspect rot, pour some wood preservative into the affected area and allow to dry. Set aside some long splints of wood (Diagram 34), maybe 6 to 8 inches long. I like to use sections of parting beads split with a chisel so they'll be roughly ½ inch by ½ inch at their thick end. The slivers will actually be long right triangles for the most part. You can also use dowels, but these seem to work better. Plus the old parting beads are free and it's one less item to purchase.

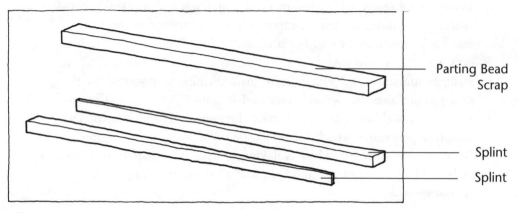

DIAGRAM 34

Mix the fill material of your choice.

Force the corner back together; if it springs apart, you can wrap a rope around the sash, knot it, and, inserting a small piece of wood or screwdriver, twist it like a tourniquet until the corner comes together (Diagram 36). Be sure they line up flush and square. Mix enough material to generously fill the cavity until it's overflowing. Then hammer your wood splints into the space and into the soft wood of the bottom rail. Believe me, they'll go right in, but don't pound so aggressively that you split the rail. You can predrill some holes if you prefer. There will be some natural resistance when you reach a stronger section of the wood. Clip the ends of the splints off until they are roughly flush with the edge of the sash and then smear some more filler over them. No need to be particularly neat about it as it will all be sanded after it dries. When the material dries hard around the splints or dowels, the whole corner will hold together, as they are now the new tenons.

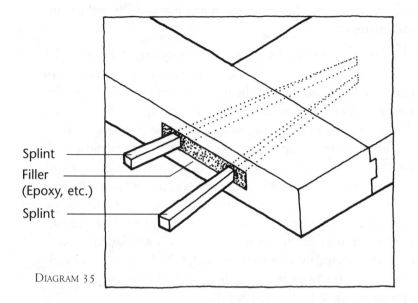

Splint
Filler
(Epoxy, etc.)
Splint

Diagram 35

Repeat the procedure at the other corner if necessary. This always works, especially if you use an epoxy. When dry, sand smooth and flush with a belt sander. Fill in any remaining cavities and sand when dry, using a finish sander to complete the job. Prime and paint the material as soon as possible in order to seal and protect it.

You can also use 16d finish nails or even deck screws instead of splints or dowels. Insert them in the same fashion and fill around them. If their heads stick out beyond the edge of the sash you can sand them off with a belt sander.

Fillers
Fillers include epoxies, wood dough, spackle, patching plasters, caulking, fiberglass-reinforced polyester resin, and automobile body compounds such as Bondo.

Wood dough, spackle, patching plasters and putty, and caulking are inappropriate for the repairs being discussed here. They are normally used for filling cracks, voids, and holes in wood and walls and not for structural repairs.

Automobile body compound consists of a polyester filler material and a hardening agent. It is quick-drying, sands easily, and is an excellent choice for wood repair. The best ones for window repair are waterproof and contain fiberglass. Swiss Glass makes such a product, although it's not always easy to find. Lightweight fillers such as Bondo are okay for these repairs, but are not as strong as those with fiberglass. Bondo does manufacture a fiberglass jelly that is excellent for this work. Fiberglass-reinforced polyester resin, according to Robert J. Albrecht (*Old House Journal*, May-June 1993), can be thinned 25 percent with acetone to soak into weakened or deteriorated wood to strengthen the fibers. He notes it is similar to soaking the wood with consolidant (see LiquidWood, below) and yields excellent results. Polyester resin is available at automotive supply stores along with automobile body compound.

When used properly, these materials are suitable for many window repairs. Proper applications include using the material on a dry sash, thoroughly packing the cavity or area to be repaired with the filler so you do not leave any gaps or voids, and allowing sufficient time for it to harden in a dry, preferably warm, area. You may have to apply the material several times to complete your repair if the cavity is deep.

Some repairers and restorers shun body fillers, claiming they are inadequate and eventually loosen and separate from the wood they are repairing. There is some truth to this, particularly if a corner of a sash has some flex to it (the stile working against the rail). For the most part, I haven't found this to be a problem.

The most foolproof material is epoxy. It is also the most time-consuming and expensive. Marine suppliers and some paint stores carry various brands of epoxy mixes. The product usually recommended by restorers is one made by Albatron, Inc. (5501 95th Ave., Kenosha, WI 53144; 1-800-445-1754). It is available direct from the manufacturer.

Albatron's LiquidWood and WoodEpox are miracle materials that can repair even the most rotted wood. LiquidWood is a two-part liquid consolidant. When mixed and poured onto deteriorated wood, LiquidWood will penetrate and harden the existing wood fibers to the point that they can be sawed, drilled, or sanded, rendering it harder than the original material. WoodEpox is a two-part structural putty used to fill large holes and voids, even to replace entire missing sections. It can also be sanded and tooled. LiquidWood can also be mixed with sawdust and used as a putty-type material. These are amazing products and work best in dry weather (they can take forever to dry in damp conditions). They can also cost four to five times as much as automotive body filler and may be a more exotic material than you really need. Albatron is very popular with historic preservationists because it can repair even the most neglected wood.

Bigger Wood Repairs
Let's assume the entire corner is gone. This can be repaired, although it requires a small act of faith. You'll proceed as above, but will have to contain the filler material until it hardens into a corner.

Dig out all of the deteriorated material and force the corner back into its proper position. This may require you crossing it in both directions with rope and tightening. On one side of the now missing corner, attach a piece of cardboard wrapped in plastic wrap to the adjoining rails using thumbtacks. Wrap the edge of the cardboard around the bottom edge of the rail so the filler won't ooze out here. The plastic wrap will prevent the filler material from sticking so the cardboard can be easily pulled away (Diagrams 36–38).

Note: The filler material, especially auto body filler, has a short life after it's mixed, only a few minutes before hardening. Work quickly!

Lay the sash on the side with the cardboard. Stuff some filler into the ends of the rails. Then hammer some splints into both rails, cut them roughly flush with the edge of the rail, and layer a little more material into and over the splints. Don't try to fill the whole corner out at once. After your first application dries, apply a second or even a third until it fills out completely. You may want to wrap an additional piece of cardboard against the edge of the sash to prevent oozing there. After the filler has dried, remove the cardboard and sand everything flush and square. You will probably need one last application to fill in small voids.

Does this work? Well, I once had to fill an entire bottom rail with pieces of parting bead, construction glue, and Bondo, making repeated applications, until I had just about re-created the entire rail. All that was left of it was the interior face, about ⅛ inch thick. I mean, it was necessary: The window had to be reinstalled that day and there wasn't any time to have a new rail made. It's still working today.

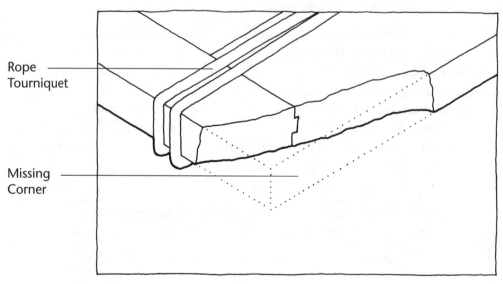

Rope Tourniquet

Missing Corner

DIAGRAM 36

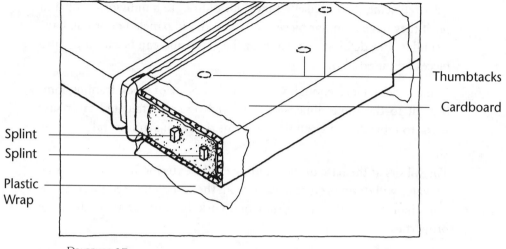

Thumbtacks

Cardboard

Splint

Splint

Plastic
Wrap

DIAGRAM 37

Completed Repair

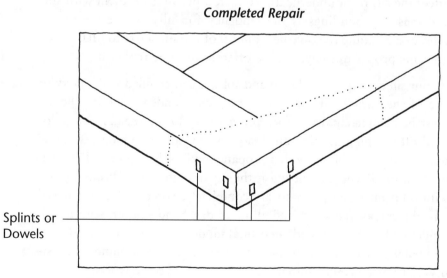

Splints or
Dowels

DIAGRAM 38

Now let's talk about rot. If the rail is just too far gone to repair, consider replacing the rail itself. Take your old rail to a millwork shop and see if they have a similar piece available. An old paneled door will have a similar ogee detail (the detail near the glass) and can be cut into scrap pieces and used also.

You can get a close-enough version with a piece of stock framing lumber cut to the same dimension followed by some talented table-saw work to reproduce a credible ogee. Cut the tenons and install.

Sills

The sill sits at the base of the window on the exterior. It is cut at a slope so water will drain off it and away from the sash. Sills need more attention than most other exterior woodwork because of their drainage properties.

When poorly maintained or left unpainted, sills will either rot or split due to weathering. Moisture is the ultimate enemy. In masonry structures, moisture can even rise up from the bricks themselves and affect the sill from underneath. In fact, a peculiar problem with sills and masonry buildings is the tendency for sills on the weathered sides of a building to cup (the front lip of the sill starts to lift), which prevents proper drainage. These often have to be replaced.

If your sill is simply weathered and split, it can be filled with epoxy or one of the various fiberglass materials and sanded smooth. The sill must be completely dry before you start to do the repairs. Scrape or sand off (keeping in mind any lead content) all loose paint. In damp weather, dry the sill out with a propane torch or heat gun and cover it with plastic if you cannot finish the repair right away. Prime the sill with oil primer and allow to dry completely. Force the filler material into the cracks and splits and allow to dry. Sand smooth with a disk sander and finish-sand with an orbital sander. Prime again immediately and paint as soon as the primer has dried. There are a number of fast-drying primers available that may be useful if you're working during damp or wet weather.

Sill replacement can be a real nuisance. The sill is nailed up and into the jamb as shown below. It is impractical to try to remove the entire window unit and renail a new sill. Usually, only a portion of the sill, maybe up to one-half of its width, deteriorates and has to be removed. This results in splicing in a new section and filling the seam between the new and old wood.

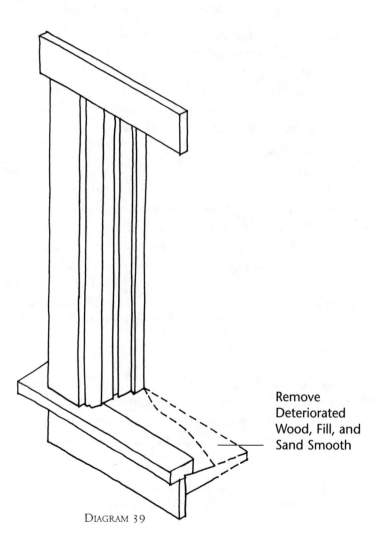

Remove Deteriorated Wood, Fill, and Sand Smooth

DIAGRAM 39

If you're only replacing a portion of a sill, you can use any number of sizes of standard dimensional lumber as long as you sand or plane it to match the slope of the original sill and bevel the front edge to match the original. It's a good idea to cut a drip line on the underside of the sill as well. This is a narrow channel, about ⅜ inch deep, cut into the sill about 2 inches from the edge and along its entire length. It helps to prevent water from accumulating under the sill.

Cut your wood to the approximate shape of the section that has been removed and prime the underside. Secure it to the undamaged section of the sill (see below for replacing large sections) with glue and either galvanized screws or finish nails. Fill in the gaps between the new and old wood with epoxy or other appropriate filler. Sand smooth when dry and prime the entire sill. Apply at least two coats of paint to finish the job.

Replacement

A deteriorated sill will be pretty obvious to you. The wood will be soft to the point where you can sink a screwdriver into it and pull it apart in large pieces. Remove all the loose, trashed wood with a hammer and chisel or circular saw. Completely clean out all pieces of the deteriorated sill that run under the jamb and exterior trim or brick molding. Note that you will have to saw off or pull out any remnants of nails sticking into the jamb from the sill. Chisel or saw the sill until you hit solid wood. Try to make your cut as smooth and even as possible so it will butt up cleanly to your new spliced-in piece.

Unfortunately, you can't just tuck a new sill piece in and call it good. Because of the angle of the sill and the framing on which it sits, the ends of the sill have to be trimmed down in order to slip under the jamb. This usually results in a gap once the sill is snugged up tight. Since you can't nail up into the jamb, you have to pound some shims under the sill to form a tight fit against the jamb. It's ultimately a compromise, but renders a very usable repair.

Again, you can use just about any dimensional lumber that fits as long as you maintain the proper slope and seal the edges at the jamb. It will probably be necessary to seal under the sill at the front edge, as your replacement piece may not sit as flat as the original. Be sure to prime the underside of your replacement piece.

Purchase new sill material (available at lumberyards) if you have to replace most of the old sill. You will have to cut down the width of the new material in order to match the dimensions of the original. How much you will have to cut off will be determined by how much of the old sill remains after the rotted or deteriorated sections have been removed.

Missing or Broken Hardware

Locks and sash lifts (handles) are commonly available at hardware and home repair centers. The least expensive are made from aluminum and come with several finishes including bright brass, antique brass, and bronze. Solid-brass hardware is very expensive and doesn't offer any clear advantages over aluminum in terms of function. It certainly feels heavier and more substantial, but at a price.

Your existing hardware may be quite usable despite the paint buildup.

Yeah, but Mr. Window, cleaning all that paint off is a real mess. Actually, it's really easy. Remove all of the hardware. Consider discarding the screws and replacing (the cheapest way to buy them is by the bag or box at a fastener supplier). Toss everything into an old coffee can (a thing that is quickly becoming an artifact, since these days everyone grinds their own coffee into cool-looking gourmet bags) or similar container along with about 1 cup of granulated dishwasher detergent. Fill the can with boiling water, cover it, and let it sit for a day. All paint will dissolve. An even better approach is to keep it all simmering or boiling in an old pot on a hot plate outdoors. If you put it on your stove, your kitchen will take on one of life's less pleasant odors. This is a very nifty tip and is good for cleaning paint off any small metal objects. Trisodium phosphate (TSP) can be used instead of dishwasher detergent, but it's more expensive. If you have an electric buffer or fine wire wheel to clean the hardware after the paint has been stripped, all the better. Otherwise, you'll have to clean it by hand with steel wool. If it's brass, you can get it as bright as a mirror.

If the hardware is still a bit plain after cleaning, apply bronze-colored spray paint. It will look great.

Note: Dispose of the wastewater properly.

Pulleys

Occasionally, a pulley breaks. If yours are held in with screws, they can be easily removed.

After some hunting around, replacements can be found. They are not a common item, but a few manufacturers still produce them. If your pulleys are not held in with screws, then they are the type that were wedged in and may have a nail passing through the center of the wheels inside the pocket. These were added as an extra precaution so the pulleys would not fall out of the jamb. If you cannot see inside the pocket, you won't know if a nail is present until you start to remove the pulley.

If this latter type is broken, and the nail is present, you'll have to remove the casing, remove the nail, and then push the pulley through from inside the pocket. Of course, if one pulley per sash operates that can be okay, too. The sash will still move, after all. Used pulleys from salvage companies dealing with architectural materials are sometimes available. Or call a company that installs new windows, inquire when they are next removing old double-hung windows, and ask if you can salvage some pulleys. They usually just hammer them into the jamb to make room for the new windows.

Problems with the Weights

Sometimes, the weights will get wedged in the pocket. There may have been a little shifting in the framing, thus restricting the space, or they may have always been tight and never worked properly. If they are only a little tight, you might try spraying a lot of lubricant down into the pocket from the pulley. Soak them with silicone or WD-40. If they are truly too tight to pass each other, put a narrower weight in to solve the problem. Sometimes just swapping with another weight in the opposite pocket will work.

If you haven't got any scrap weights or any that are narrow enough, you can make one out of old pipe filled with concrete or similar material. Just cap one end, pour or push the material of choice down the other end, and place an "eye" in the still-wet material. This will provide a place to tie the rope. Test that everything clears before installing the sash.

Casement Hinges

If you have butt hinges, soak them to remove the paint, spray them with a rust-inhibiting primer, repaint, and reinstall. If you have friction hinges that are frozen, strip them as well. If they don't improve much, hold them over a gas flame or propane torch. This usually loosens them up. Spray the bottom hinge with rust inhibitor and lubricate both hinges by soaking them in a shallow container of oil or penetrating oil overnight and then wiping clean.

Note: If you replace one or both of the hinges, replace them with the same-size hinge! Measure the hinge in its closed position. (It will be 8, 10, or 12 inches in length or some such derivation.) A new hinge will affect the way the sash opens, even if it is the same size as the old hinge. Don't ask me why, it just does. Maybe because the manufacturers are different. After installing a new hinge, you may have to trim the sash down slightly so it will close properly.

Sloppy or Tight Fit

Double-Hung Windows

It's a good idea to check for fit before installing the parting beads. Do this by installing the upper sash and raising it completely. Then install the lower sash; be sure it's as straight as it would be if it were resting against the parting bead, and observe how well the sash match up at the meeting rail and how well they slide. You can also tap small scraps of parting bead into the jamb and hold the sash against them.

With a double-hung window, you'll know if it's too tight as you install the ropes and move the sash up and down. If the upper sash is tight as it slides down, remove the paint from the exterior jamb. If it's still tight, or if the lower sash is tight, then it's a matter of taking a belt sander to the sides of the sash and gradually trimming away. Don't get carried away with the sander. Sand some and then test the sash in the opening.

If the sash slides easily until the parting bead is installed, then try to force the parting bead in farther, as it may be sticking out too far.

If the sash are too loose, see if adding weather stripping will resolve the problem. If they are way loose, you'll have to add a wood shim to the side of the sash. Measure the gap and slice off a shim by running a piece of lumber through a table saw. Or buy a bullnose stop or a piece of lattice the same width as the thickness of the sash and close to the additional size you need to add. Cut a slot in it to match the groove in the side of the sash to accommodate the rope. The material available will probably be wider than the sash is thick and will have to be trimmed down. You can also just build up the very edges of the sash with narrower material, like a parting bead cut in half lengthwise.

If the sash do not meet properly at the meeting rail, you may have to add a shim to one sash. It's easiest to add to the upper rail of the upper sash. If the sash bypass each other (that is, one is too big and they cannot be locked), you will have to trim one or both sash until they do meet. Again, it's easier to trim the top rail of the upper sash. If they are only off slightly or you do not want to do any trimming, you can always add a small shim under one section of the lock until they do lock together.

Casement Windows

Like humans, casement windows begin to lose their shape as they age. Typically, they sag against the hinged side, particularly with butt hinges. As their shape changes, casements will no longer open and close properly, often sticking against the jamb. If they have been shut for years and are then sprung open, they often will not close without being trimmed down.

Before doing any extreme hacking, remove the sash and all the paint from its edges. Then strip the paint from the window jamb. This combination may be sufficient adjustment for the window to close easily.

When reinstalling, be sure the hinge screws are tight. A small amount of play can throw the sash off and prevent it from closing completely.

If stripping the paint isn't sufficient, try to close the sash and note where it is sticking out beyond the edge of the jamb. This is almost always on the stile opposite the hinge side, that is, the edge with the lock. Look up and down the length of the sash as you close it. On the interior face of the sash, mark the sections that need trimming with a pencil. To do this, close the sash as far as it will go and run the pencil down the jamb, drawing a line on the face of the sash.

After marking, trim the side of the sash with a plane, a scraper (a regular paint scraper, not the Red Devil carbide scraper), or a sander (Diagram 40). Do this a bit at a time and close the sash after each trimming. You only want to remove a small amount of wood. Eventually, the sash will close tautly. Trim enough so it will close easily and not scrape any paint from the jamb. There should be enough room between the sash and the jamb, after painting, to insert a business card or a flexible putty knife. You may need more room if you are installing weather stripping.

Sometimes the hinged edge or the stile opposite the lock will stick on the inner edge of the jamb, before you can barely close it. It would seem to work okay if the whole sash could be pushed outward another ⅛ inch or so, but if you did this it would not sit well in the jamb. If this is the case, you will have to trim the edge of the sash that is hitting at a 45-degree angle until it will pass freely. Usually, a piece of coarse-grit sandpaper or a file will do the job. Just run either one up and down the edge until you put a slight bevel on it. Casement adjustment is more an art than a science so you have to do whatever works.

Occasionally a casement will stick at the upper rail. If so, sand it lightly until it closes. More often, though, the bottom rail will not clear at the sill. The easiest way to trim here is to run a belt sander against the bottom side of the rail, doing a small amount at a time. Close after each sanding and check for clearance.

Note: Almost all old casement windows feature a single lock, located in the middle of one of the stiles. Two locks are better because they would prevent the bottom of the sash from migrating out away from the jamb. Once again, those clever builders saved maybe fifty cents per window by not installing a second lock. Also, without a second lock near the bottom of the sash, you may not be able to determine how far to trim. What may appear to be a sticking sash that will not close all the way could actually be a slightly warped sash that needs to be pulled in near the bottom. I'm a big advocate of additional locks, especially on tall casements. You can either locate a second lock near the bottom rail or remove the original lock and locate it and the other lock an equal distance from the top and bottom of the sash.

Another way of pulling in the sash at the bottom is to install a handle or hook lift, although these may not be as elegant-looking as a second lock.

If Your Casement Is Weather-Stripped

Interlocking weather stripping was the material of choice used with casement windows. Like its double-hung counterparts, this material must line up properly in order to close and seal completely. If the

DIAGRAM 40

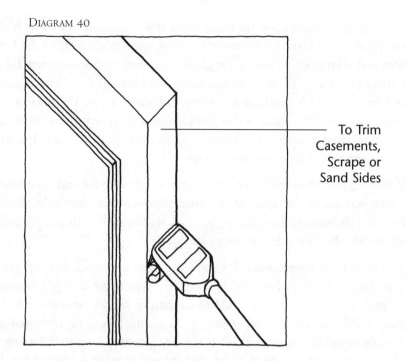

To Trim
Casements,
Scrape or
Sand Sides

casement has misformed over the years, it may be that the weather stripping will not line up and should be removed. You may only have to remove some sections of it.

If the weather stripping is loose, renail it with small wire nails (with heads) or copper weather-stripping nails. A ¾ inch size will do nicely. Also, set any loose nails. Observe where the weather stripping is binding and bend its opposing pieces outward with a wide putty knife a bit at a time. If they simply will not lock together, remove the section from the jamb. You can pry it off or drive the nails through with a nail set or punch. Spring bronze or vinyl weather stripping (see "Weather Stripping," pages 91–95) can be installed in its place.

Fixed Windows
Fixed windows have some peculiar problems. Let's start with single fixed sash.

The larger the fixed sash, the more likely it will migrate out away from the jamb (if it's installed from the outside), most noticeably at the bottom rail. Typically, as the space grows, painters or homeowners fill it with caulk or spackle or other fun stuff. The glass also tends to migrate out from the sash itself, at the bottom. I don't know the reason for either of these phenomena other than some shifting or movement in the building itself, gravity, or possibly alien anti-window rays that are being directed at us from outer space.

If this separation bothers you or is extreme, remove the sash and reset. Clean out all of the spackle or other filler material formerly placed between the sash and the jamb. You can set the sash with countersunk screws on the side stiles for extra security.

The glass is another matter. It can be removed and reset, but old glass is fragile, so it has to be removed carefully. Removing a large pane can be precarious. If it's secure and has enough space on the outside to be glazed, I'd suggest leaving it unless it's really loose. Be prepared to replace the glass, though. If it's quite large, it may be worth having a glazier remove it, although he or she will not guarantee against breakage during removal or resetting.

If you have a fixed sash that was installed from the outside, it can usually be made operable as either a casement or awning type, depending on its size. Just install the appropriate hardware.

Double-Hung Fixed Windows
If they're intact and you don't want them to open, then leave them. If you want them to open, you have several options.

If there is a pocket space in the wall, you can install ropes, pulleys, and weights, if you have some spare parts. Remove the casing and any underlying plaster and lath, drill through the jamb, and install the pulleys. Proceed with the ropes and weights. If the side of the sash has not been routed and drilled for rope installation, you will have to do this as well.

Your window may not have any pocket space, that is, it may be up against a wall stud. In this case, you can install duplex pulleys.

The *easiest* solution, however, is to install sash controls or sash pins. Granted, they won't be as smooth as other hardware, but simplicity has its benefits. I would say that if the windows surrounding or near a fixed double-hung window are operating, then there is little reason to render the fixed window operable; but if you need more ventilation in the room, then by all means open it.

WEATHER STRIPPING

Weather stripping is available in the following general categories:

- ✓ Spring bronze
- ✓ Interlocking
- ✓ Vinyl
- ✓ Foam

Spring Bronze

Spring bronze is a thin brass weather stripping available in various widths. A crease in the material prevents it from lying flat and it is forced against the side of a sash or door (therein the "spring"), forming a seal against drafts. This is the most versatile, long-lasting, and forgiving material available. It adapts to almost all sizes of gaps and misaligned windows. Pemko manufactures a high-quality product. The most commonly available material is 1⅛ inches and comes in 17-foot rolls (enough for one door). Longer rolls can be ordered. Although this is an acceptable size for residential windows, I prefer 1½ inches (for double-hung windows only; it won't fit residential-size casements), as it gives a cleaner appearance. This must be ordered from the factory. I buy it in 100-foot rolls, each one of which is enough to do ten to twelve windows.

Spring bronze material can be installed with either nails or staples. A good electric stapler is a big help if you're installing a lot of it. Use galvanized staples, as the brass-colored ones can rust. If you go to rent a stapler, take a piece of the weather stripping and an old board with you and test that the stapler is strong enough to punch the staples through the metal. If you order the 1½-inch Pemko and want to use nails, these must be ordered separately. The more common size, 1⅛ inches, includes nails in the packaging. I have found that the heads on these can corrode, too.

When installing the spring bronze at the meeting rail, the nailing edge should face up (Diagrams 41–42). Allow a little room at the far ends so it won't scrape the parting bead as the sash slides. Installed at the jamb, this edge should face toward the room so the flared edge forms a seal to the outside.

At the lower sash, you can measure and cut the spring bronze so it's flush with the top of the lower sash and the bottom of the upper, I prefer to run it about 1 inch longer. This way, if the edge of the sash is a bit rough and catches the end of the weather stripping, you can add a nail or staple at this corner (this is opposite the nailing edge, the edge that normally flares out) and not lose any of the seal because this end runs out beyond the sash. Is that clear? Probably not, but trust me, it's a good idea.

After you have installed the weather stripping, slowly run the sash up and down to check for rough spots or catching at the end of the spring bronze. If you can smooth out the spot on the sash, fine. If not, nail the edge of the weather stripping where it's catching. When installing at the upper sash, you'll have to cut the material to fit around the pulley (or install vinyl as noted below).

Spring bronze works quite well with casement windows. The nailing edge should face outside, however, so the sash closes against the flared edge. If you have butt hinges, you can run the material right over the hinges, although some believe that spring bronze on this edge of the sash will throw it out of alignment because it's constantly

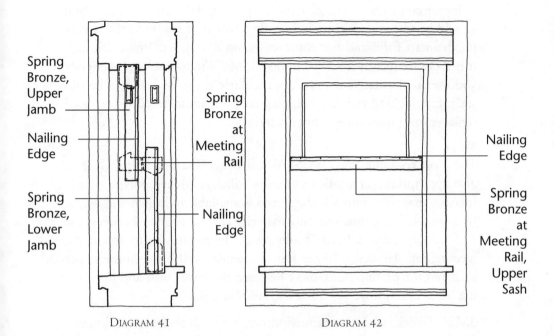

Spring Bronze, Upper Jamb

Nailing Edge

Spring Bronze, Lower Jamb

Spring Bronze at Meeting Rail

Nailing Edge

Nailing Edge

Spring Bronze at Meeting Rail, Upper Sash

DIAGRAM 41

DIAGRAM 42

forcing it away. Sometimes it does, sometimes it doesn't. If you have friction hinges, you can only partially weather-strip the upper jamb and at the sill.

There is some debate around installing spring bronze on the sill because it may prevent any water, which can blow in during a storm, from draining. Also, it tends to get covered with a lot of paint over the years and looks kind of wretched. If I find a gap between the bottom rail and the stool, I normally install a narrow, flat piece of molding on the stool and right up against the sash. Sometimes I'll install a piece of foam weather stripping on its edge to butt up against the sash.

Interlocking

I have never installed interlocking weather stripping in a new window or in an old sash that did not already have weather stripping. Weather-stripping contractors, like glaziers, are part of life's natural balance and should be recognized as such. Installing this stuff from scratch is very much an art form and few contractors install it in windows, although it is more frequently installed in doors. Mr. Window strongly suggests you use an alternative material, particularly if you're dealing with old sash. Interlocking weather stripping is still manufactured if you need replacement pieces for existing material.

Vinyl

The most common vinyl is 3M V-Seal Door Weather Strip, which is also appropriate for windows. This is adhesive-backed polypropylene (plastic) that folds into a V shape and is available in brown and white. In a double-hung window, this material can be pressed between the sash and the parting bead (it adheres to the parting bead) and at the meeting rail. However, I have found it works well between the upper sash and the parting bead, okay between the lower sash and the parting bead, and not well at all at the meeting rail.

3M also works with casement windows, but I still prefer spring bronze. The 3M requires a very clean surface, preferably unpainted, for the adhesive to stick. It sticks well to new parting beads, but not as well to old casement jambs.

With double-hung windows, I usually combine the 3M and the Pemko, using the spring bronze at the meeting rail and between the jamb and the lower sash, and the 3M at the upper sash. Pemko also makes a V vinyl weather stripping at a lower cost than 3M.

Foam

Foam weather stripping is available in different thicknesses and widths. Two types are manufactured: closed-cell, a thick, dense material; and open-cell, which is less dense, lighter, and more pliable. Neither type works well in double-hung windows and their performance varies with casements and doors. The closed-cell is less flexible, so if it is thicker than the gap you are trying to seal, the window (or door) will not close properly.

Other Materials

There are other types of rigid weather stripping available for doors that, in some instances, can be used for windows. You may have gaps or problems that defy the usual choice of materials. These other types consist of lengths of aluminum with a vinyl bead on one edge. The installer cuts them to length and screws or nails them to the door jamb. They can also be nailed to double-hung window stops or to casement jambs. I have even nailed them at meeting rails when the situation called for it. There is also a flexible roll of metal with a felt edge available.

Because of its material (metal and vinyl), this type of weather stripping is industrial-looking, but it does the job. Your local hardware store will carry some selection of weather stripping, but a wholesale hardware company will carry more contractor-grade material, so check this out as well.

REPAINTING, REFINISHING

Painting and finishing of sash and windows is a million times easier if the window is disassembled. Some touch-up and caulking will be needed after assembly. You can even paint the outside casings and sill with the sash out, a real plus if you don't like working off ladders.

The following is Mr. Window's crash course on painting and finishing to complete your window repair work.

Paint

Once upon a time, paint was oil-based. That is, it contained oil, usually linseed, paint thinner, color pigment, and other fun stuff. Some old-time painters swear by it, waxing especially nostalgic about lead-based paint. "Best damn paint you could get, you know. Never should have stopped making it." Yeah, well, life changes.

Once again, the wonderful world of chemistry improved our lives with latex paint, which is water-based. All this means is that the water in the paint maintains it as a liquid until it evaporates. You apply the paint, the water evaporates (or the thinner in the case of oil-based paint), and the remaining ingredients harden into a protective film.

Which is better? Depends on the application and with whom you consult. At some point in the near future the question will be a moot one because oil-based paint and finishes are gradually being phased out and will probably be available only for limited, specialized uses. The first generation of latex paint left something to be desired, particularly for use on woodwork. The current material is vastly improved and is used for myriad applications. Many painters used to prefer latex for walls and oil for woodwork, although in new construction latex is used on everything.

Before you paint, all bare surfaces will need an application of primer. Primer's purpose in life is to seal up bare wood and act as an acceptable surface for paint to adhere to. It is not the same as paint, nor does it offer the same degree of protection.

Although oil-based paint tends to stick to most surfaces well, latex will not stick to glossy surfaces previously painted with oil paint. These surfaces must be completely deglossed (I prefer to do this by sanding). An application of primer after deglossing will usually give the latex a better bonding surface. If you paint directly over glossy oil paint with latex, the latter has the wonderful tendency of flaking off with the least bit of encouragement, such as bumping a chair or vacuum cleaner against the woodwork.

If you paint your sash while they're disassembled, go ahead and paint all the sides of casement, awning, and fixed sash, but *prime only* the edges of double-hung windows. If you paint these, they tend to squeal when they run up against the painted jamb.

If your woodwork is stained and varnished and you wish to refinish, remove and clean as much of the old finish off as possible. Stains, for coloring the wood, come both oil-based and latex-based. I prefer the oil-based, but these will probably be slowly phased out.

After staining, you should apply a clear finish material. You may even choose to skip the stain and use a clear finish over the stripped wood. A clear finish provides a protective film. Otherwise, the wood becomes stained from fingerprints, spilled drinks, dog drool, etc. Clear finishes include shellac, oil, lacquer, varnish, and polyurethane.

Shellac is an ancient finish that has some unique properties, but is rarely used on woodwork anymore. Forget about it unless you're doing some specific matching that requires the use of orange shellac. Oils, unless you use pure tung oil, are essentially diluted varnishes/polyurethanes, and look great after first applied, but don't offer much protection unless periodically reapplied. They are easy to use for homeowners and are thus quite popular. If you use them, apply several coats until a decent film forms. Lacquer is very fast-drying and has to be sprayed. Forget this one, too, unless you're doing a ton of woodwork and want to practice your spraying techniques.

Varnish and polyurethane are clear finishes that form protective films, particularly after two or three applications. Basically, varnish has a natural resin and polyurethane a synthetic one, although the distinctions have become blurred. Both are oil-based, although water-based polyurethanes are now available and, again, are the wave of the future. These finishes, in their oil form, are slow-drying, so allow twelve hours per coat to cure. Because of this long drying time, they are susceptible to dust and other floating material landing and sticking on them. Be sure your work area is very clean and well vacuumed. If you're working during the winter months or damp weather, keep the house warm, but keep the furnace ducts only partially open in your work area so the dust doesn't blow around too much.

Paint, varnish, and polyurethane have different degrees of gloss in their finish. High-gloss is the shiniest, followed by semigloss, satin, and flat. Flat finishes don't clean as easily as the others. High-gloss might be a bit much unless you like to think you're living on a boat, marine finishes traditionally being very bright.

How do you apply your finish? For latex or oil, buy the appropriate brush. Throwaway foam brushes have limited use and are not good for detail work, such as painting near the glass. Cheap brushes lose bristles, which end up in your finish work. A good brush holds more paint and saves time. This does not mean you need a twenty-five-dollar varnishing brush from your local wooden boat store, but do ask the clerk at the paint store to recommend what a painting contractor would use. The investment is minor and worth it.

Paint in long strokes, with your final ones being very light, just enough to even out the paint with the ends of the bristles. Generally, work the horizontal surfaces first and the vertical ones last. If you have any drips, try to correct them early. As the finish dries, attempts to brush them out can leave an imperfection in the finished product.

Follow the recommended drying times for your chosen finish. If applying more than one coat (except for clear oil), lightly sand between coats with 220 sandpaper or finer. Wipe off the dust with a tack cloth.

After reinstalling the sash, caulk where needed, such as at the stops or the jamb of a fixed sash. Touch up the paint as needed.

CHAPTER FIVE

MOLDINGS

MOLDINGS AND CASING STYLES

Moldings are simply decorative pieces of wood used for transitions from one surface to another (a floor to a wall, for instance). They also provide a degree of protection. Baseboards, which run at the bottom of a wall and rest on the floor, prevent plaster and paint from being nicked by vacuum cleaners, furniture legs, and toy trucks. Door casings, which run around a door frame or jamb, prevent the corners or edges of walls from being chipped. Picture molding was installed so pictures could be hung from it rather than being secured by nails or hangers pounded into the walls (although later on, in the 1920s and 1930s, it was installed for mostly decorative purposes).

In a sense, you can document social and economic changes by the types and size of woodwork in American homes. In grander eighteenth- and nineteenth-century American homes, baseboards could be 16 to 18 inches wide with additional trim on top and a wide baseshoe. Ceilings in these homes were quite tall, up to 10 feet or so, which almost required a wide baseboard, and wider door and window trim, to offer a sense of proportion. Trees were everywhere and the locals weren't using them to build casinos yet. As the years progressed, and presumably demand increased and a supply of readily available trees diminished, woodwork gradually shrank until you had the whopping 1½-inch finger-jointed baseboards of today's homes. Economics probably dictated shrinking dimensions more than fashion. As baseboards narrowed, ceiling heights were lowered while Americans were gradually getting taller. Maybe the early colonists and settlers had a massive Napoleon complex.

Going into the 1800s, moldings were rendered by hand planing. Special molding planes produced a variety of patterns and styles. The results were very labor-intensive and consequently were not found in common homes. Life would have been a lot simpler if Black & Decker had been around (okay, electricity would have been helpful, too). Sawmills, where available, basically did rough cutting. Smoothing and shaping required skilled hand labor and a lot of it. Even flat boards were planed and smoothed by hand.

Toward the end of the nineteenth century and certainly into the twentieth, even the most basic homes featured some kind of trim around doors, windows, and floors. This was evidence of cheaper production costs (boards could now be machined for smoothing and shaping) and a rising gentrification, no matter how humble its manifestations. A simpler or less expensive home may have been given only plain boards for baseboards and casings, but they were present nevertheless.

Since woodwork and molding don't perform any mechanical functions (opening and closing), the main issue you'll deal with as a homeowner is refinishing or repainting. As with window sash, you will have to remove the old finish or prepare it for painting. Like sash, woodwork can be removed, which is sometimes a good idea. First, a short history lesson on carpentry and finishes.

Once upon a time, carpentry, like many trades, didn't exactly qualify its practitioners to become members of the Forbes 400 wealthiest Americans. Now, with more and more people spending their days in front of computer monitors, carpenters and contractors can rightfully demand higher fees for their labor for doing work that everyone's grandfather used to be able to do as a matter of course. Up until the 1940s (by my observations), carpenters followed the *lots-o'-nails* philosophy of finish carpentry. If they needed eight nails to secure a piece of trim, they used fifteen. As I mentioned earlier, they must have gotten paid by the nail. This will affect how you remove your woodwork should you decide to do so. Fortunately, these guys didn't have automatic nailing guns.

In the 1920s, clever carpenters introduced the neat trick of nailing up through the stool of a window into the vertical painted casings as shown below. Mitered horizontal casings would be nailed both to the wall and down and into the vertical casings they butted up against, also shown below. This was very thorough, very unnecessary, and very annoying to anyone trying to remove the trim.

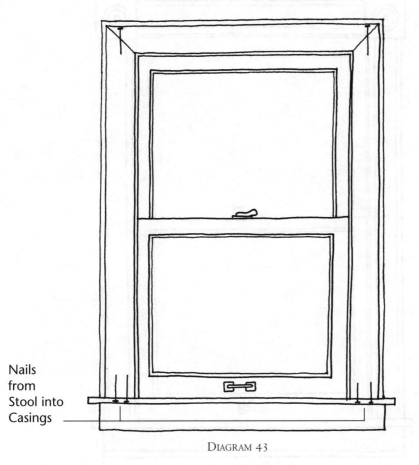

Nails Through Mitered Corner

Nails from Stool into Casings

Diagram 43

Other styles of window casings were also assembled in their own unique fashion. Victorian structures built at the end of the nineteenth century typically had bull's-eye pieces where vertical and head (horizontal) casings met over doors and windows. The bull's-eyes, as shown below, were often overnailed and can split during removal, although they are easily reglued.

Victorian-Style Woodwork

DIAGRAM 44

A common casing style around the turn of the century consisted of a cap molding, a head casing, a fillet or bullnose trim, and vertical casings. The fillet was nailed down and into the vertical casings and sometimes up and into the head casing in the center with one or two nails. The illustration below shows the most common locations for nails.

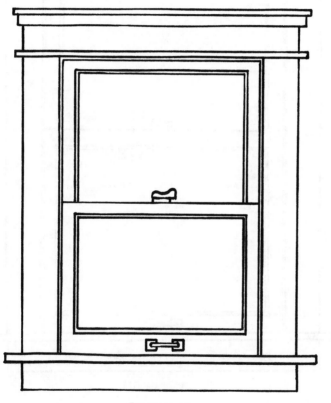

DIAGRAM 45

Some styles were plainer, without the fillet, but simply a head casing with ends cut at 45-degree angles, as shown in Diagram 46.

45°-Angle Casings

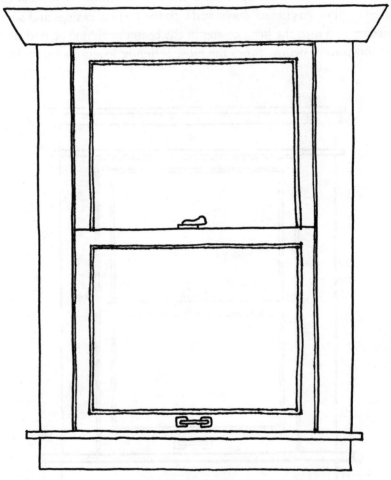

DIAGRAM 46

Finishes varied depending on the era and, to a lesser extent, geography. Shellac was often used in the late 1800s and early 1900s, with and without a wood stain for color. The same for varnish, although the color of choice seems to have been a dark walnut oil stain. Kitchens and bathrooms were typically painted starting in the early

1900s. In the 1920s, almost all woodwork was painted with the general exception of brick Tudors. As a rule, these houses would have varnished mahogany woodwork in the entry, dining, and living rooms, and a varnished staircase, railing, newel posts, and spindles. The second floor, kitchen, and bathrooms would normally have painted woodwork. Milk paint, an inexpensive alternative to oil-based paint, was sometimes used prior to this century. Ever vigilant to the problems of paint-induced corpulence, milk paint was made from nonfat milk. I suppose to remove it you need to mix crushed cookies with solvent.

REFINISHING AND REMOVAL

If you have your heart set on refinishing your woodwork, do a small sample piece first to test the results! Different finishes strip off with varying degrees of effort. You may or may not find the results to your liking. If the original finish is either shellac or varnish, then you have a decent chance of stripping it clean and refinishing, regardless of whether it's been painted over or not.

If your woodwork has always been painted, however, stripping it will be a long, Zen journey: a lot of work, a lot of patience, and an ultimate encounter with the theory of solipsism (which states that you cannot know anything other than your own thoughts, feelings, or perceptions, and that's all you'll be left with after your spouse, children, and dog move out). Try as you may, you will never get this woodwork clean enough to stain and coat with a clear finish. Strip a small section. Scrub it with solvent and sand it smooth. Then go over it with a wet rag and watch small bits of primer show up, buried away in the grain of the wood. This will always happen in shaped molding.

If you really have your heart set on unpainted woodwork, consider replacing it. A millwork company can reproduce any known pattern for a price. There will be a setup fee for every order or run so be sure to have all your measurements for the entire project and run everything at once.

Note: If you choose to replace your woodwork, bear in mind what you cannot realistically replace unless you want to start tearing your house up. Just stripping the window casings may look too odd, so you have to keep going. This would include the doors, door jambs, window sash, and window jambs. You can compromise and replace your casings and baseboards, and grain the remaining wood to match the unpainted wood. Graining is covered on page 112.

Refinishing woodwork can be a messy procedure. If it has never been painted and only has varnish or shellac on it, your chore is relatively simple. Paint over varnish or shellac can be *very* messy depending on the number of coats of paint and the intricacies of the woodwork. I generally advocate removing painted woodwork with the exception of wide baseboards (anything over 4 inches). Removing casings and moldings is not an intimidating process and can give you cleaner results than stripping in place.

How do you remove it? Follow the procedures for removing window casings as noted on page 34. If you want to practice, remove a casing from inside a closet. Just be certain you insert a wide, flat, chisel-type putty knife between the wood and the wall or the jamb, and pry it out slightly each time. Continue to do this, gradually pulling out a little farther. Then insert a pry bar for the final removal.

If you have to remove a fillet (Diagram 47), loosen the head casing first and pry it out from the wall, starting at the top. Move it back and forth a few times and the nail from the fillet into the bottom of the casing will loosen, allowing you to pull the casing off. Next, remove the fillet from the vertical casings and proceed to remove them as well.

And don't even think about removing door or window jambs!! Can you remove them? Sure, what went in can come out, but you'll regret it. Each jamb was fitted to its individual location and then shimmed in

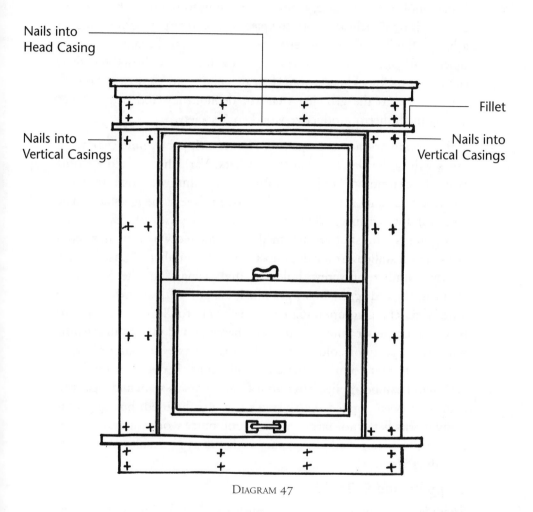

Nails into Head Casing

Fillet

Nails into Vertical Casings

Nails into Vertical Casings

DIAGRAM 47

place so it was straight and level. Strip them in place and be sure to install the door and sash that go with them.

Mark or otherwise tag the woodwork that you do remove!! Make a map so you know where it goes. Mark the jambs and locations as well.

It may look the same size, from one window to the next, but casings can be off by ⅛ inch or so. All the pieces around any window make up a happy family and if you separate them they can become very dysfunctional. Then you'll have noxious TV talk show hosts and their camera crews knocking on your door demanding to know why you are contributing to the growing trend of delinquency and petty crimes among the hitherto productive woodwork society.

If the woodwork has been painted, but is strippable, note that some areas will be harder to clean than others. Varnished window stools typically deteriorate and any subsequent paint will soak into the wood, but usually sands out easily enough. The same is usually true with window casings, which will have had a series of shades, curtains, blinds, and shutters attached and removed when the next covering was installed. You can almost trace the number of past owners by the number of screw holes in the casings. As the hardware changes, the old screw holes get filled, usually with spackle or some kind of patching compound. The easiest way to clean the fillers out is with a nail set or punch. Tap with a hammer and then refill the hole with wood putty or color putty, which is a wax-type material available in different colors to match wood stains. It does not need finishing and can be applied after your finish coats of stain and clear top coat have been applied. Putty sticks can also be used, but the color putty works better for larger holes. Wood putty works okay, but does not take the stain and clear coats with the same results as the surrounding wood.

Stripping and Refinishing

There is a variety of paint and varnish removers on the market now. Some are environmentally more sensitive (i.e., relatively useless) than standard methylene chloride remover. Others can leave stains on the stripped wood and need to be neutralized. Without wishing to sound like an anti–stripper technology Luddite, I would stick with something like original Jasco, which has evil methylene chloride in it and requires solvent for a thorough rinse (lacquer thinner, another evil substance, works very well for this purpose; if you're cleaning off shellac, dena-tured alcohol is best as a final rinse).

There are paint removers like Peel Away, which does wonders in very specific applications. It is essentially lye in a paste form and can dis-color woodwork even after being neutralized. I wouldn't recommend it for interior use. When used, it needs to be thoroughly rinsed off according to instructions. Peel Away and related products will eat through multiple layers of paint when properly applied, and clean up easily. Use only on exterior wood you're going to repaint.

For interior finishes that are varnished, simply apply the remover of your choice (you already know my choice) with an old paintbrush according to directions, scrape off the flat areas with a standard putty knife, and clean the intricate moldings with steel wool. Apply a second, lighter coat of stripper if necessary and clean everything off with steel wool dipped in lacquer thinner. Wipe clean with a rag dipped in lac-quer thinner as a final rinse. If the varnish is very thick and the first coat of stripper starts to dry out too soon, immediately apply more over it. You want to keep the remover wet so it will keep working. Use a medium grade of steel wool (the very coarse grade tends to catch on every possible splinter). For intricate work, paint stores sell brass brushes for cleaning out detailed grooves and such.

Note: Line the floor area with plastic and put a drop cloth on top of it. Wear old shoes that you can slip off easily if you have to walk off the drop cloth and onto a finished floor or carpet. Wear long rubber gloves (elbow-length) and eye protection. Use a respirator with cartridges rated for organic vapors, which are available at a safety equipment store or sometimes at a paint store. Throw all the old steel wool and gunk and rags into a disposable container like a plastic yogurt container and let them dry out.

It may only be necessary to do some minor refinishing and touch-up on your woodwork. As mentioned, the window stools and some areas of the sash (the top of the upper rail on the lower sash, the bottom rail on the upper sash, and some areas near the glass) may have deteriorated varnish due to lack of maintenance and exposure to sunlight. These areas can be sanded, stained, and recoated with a clear finish material without redoing all of the surrounding woodwork. Often the old finish is so deteriorated that it will turn into a powder as you sand it.

If you want to avoid repainting your walls when you're stripping your windows in place, be sure to put several layers of wide masking tape on the plaster, right up next to the woodwork. Use blue masking tape, which is manufactured with a longer-lasting adhesive that does not dry out as quickly as regular masking tape. Painters use this for masking work because it can be pulled away twenty-four hours after use and not leave a sticky residue or pull paint off the surface it's adhering to. Then carefully apply your stripper, especially overhead.

Painted woodwork that has been removed can be stripped pretty quickly if the majority of the paint is scraped off first down to the varnish, but not just any scraper will do. Red Devil makes a wonderful carbide scraper (see page 64) that offers superb control with less chance of gouging the wood. Scrape the worst of the paint off and then apply your paint remover. If you want it to soak in a while, apply a heavy application and cover it with plastic or even aluminum foil to keep it from drying out.

Note: Once again, the ugly specter of lead paint stares you in the face with the same leering eye as King Kong looking at Fay Wray, except you won't be carried up to the top of the Empire State Building. If you scrape off lead paint or otherwise remove it, you should be aware of its potential hazards and the proper procedures for removing and disposing of it. I've hopped out of an airplane (well, more correctly, flung myself out) and bungee-jumped off a bridge, but there's no way Mr. Window is going to stick his neck out and try to provide accurate legal information involving lead paint. My own experience has been that the rules and their enforcement are somewhat fluid, which is fine if the fluid isn't being dumped on you. Call your local air quality control office or the EPA for guidelines.

Tank stripping is also a consideration. Please see pages 63–64 for a discussion of this process.

There is one finish used in the 1920s that, in the opinion of Mr. Window, is particularly wretched-looking. It was a glaze effect, produced by applying a very thin coat of paint (diluted with mineral spirits or turpentine) as a wash coat and then wiping it off with a rag, leaving a hazy look to the wood. The woodwork was then sealed with shellac or possibly varnish. This just looks *bad* and is well worth painting over, historical purity aside.

Painting, Finishing, Graining

If you decide to repaint your woodwork, bear in mind the following: All homes built prior to the introduction of latex paint had some other type of paint applied to the painted woodwork. Even after the introduction of latex, painters used oil-based paint on the trim, inside and out. Latex in its nascent days just wasn't very durable. Now, latex is used for just about everything and oil-based paint will soon be a memory. Your woodwork may have last been painted with oil-based paint. If you plan to use latex, you will have to completely degloss the old finish and, preferably, apply a coat of oil primer to give the latex something to bite into. I prefer doing the deglossing by sanding, but this raises lead-dust issues. There are liquid deglossers available, but nothing quite beats mechanical sanding, which also smoothes out all the old brush marks. You can also use oil paint, which is still available, but is more tedious to apply and clean up. It also has a longer drying time and tends to pick up and hold any dust or dirt floating around. This is a main reason it's no longer used on new construction, where speed is paramount. If you really want to do a totally cool job, spray the woodwork with oil. This is a ton of work, though, and if you have kids, probably not worth it, since they'll eventually knock stuff into it, chipping away at your perfect, awesome woodwork.

Finishes for unpainted woodwork are discussed on pages 96–98. Apply at least three coats of your chosen material, allowing for it to thoroughly dry as noted in the directions on the can. Varnishes and polyurethanes should be lightly sanded between coats and then cleaned with a tack cloth. *Do a sample piece first!* Take that piece around to different rooms at different times of the day. The oak stain that looks so warm and cozy at high noon may be too dark and foreboding in the evening. A good rule of thumb is to go one shade lighter than your first choice.

Graining is a technique that duplicates the grain and appearance of different varieties of wood. An associated technique, marbling, reproduces the appearance of marble or other types of stone. A number of books and articles have been written on these techniques. A base coat of material is applied to the wood or metal surface being painted. This is then covered with a colored material, usually a specific type of paint, which is applied with special tools, brushes, rags, even feathers. The results can be remarkably close to the real thing. Earlier in this chapter, when it was proposed that some woodwork (casings, trim, baseboards, etc.) could be replaced, but some would have to remain (sash, door and window jambs, doors), it was suggested that the old wood be grained to match any new wood to be finished unpainted. This combination can be done very successfully and economically.

CHAPTER SIX

—— WEIRD WINDOWS, LEADED GLASS

WEIRD WINDOWS

Once in a while, I run across some strange old hardware or track system and have to improvise the repairs. Some of these systems are retrofits, that is, the original pulleys and weights may have been discarded in favor of a plastic track system that would allow the sash to tilt in for easier cleaning.

These are okay, except they're just about impossible to repair once the hardware starts breaking unless the original installer was clever enough to leave some extra parts with the building owner. Fat chance. One redeeming feature about pulleys and weights is that they can always be repaired.

I have worked on two types of pivoting windows (Diagrams 48 and 49), one with pivoting pins on the vertical stiles and one with them on the horizontal rails. The vertical ones are easy to deal with. The sash has a steel pin in the center of each stile. This pin fits into a corresponding piece of hardware installed in the jamb. The sash simply rotates on these pins. They are removed by lifting them out of the jamb hardware.

The horizontal ones, however, are terrible. Some have a crank located in the center of the bottom rail. You rotate the crank and the entire sash lifts up about 2 inches or so. It is now free to swing out on its center pivots, one attached to its top rail and one at the bottom. These windows have about the stupidest design imaginable. Depending on their size, you almost need a crane to remove them.

These windows can be repaired using the same techniques as casement windows, but if you can avoid removing them, all the better. I once did an eight-story building full of these windows without removing any of them. I trimmed and adjusted them in place and secured the loose bottom rails. The exterior stripping and painting was done by a painting contractor. Of course, I tied all of the tools off and was totally paranoid about dropping so much as a loose screw to the sidewalk below. Never again.

Some of these do not have the crank system, but simply push out. They never seal well at the stool and are generally haphazard. I suppose the original appeal to them was their ease in cleaning, because the exterior side swings around to the interior. They're still stupid.

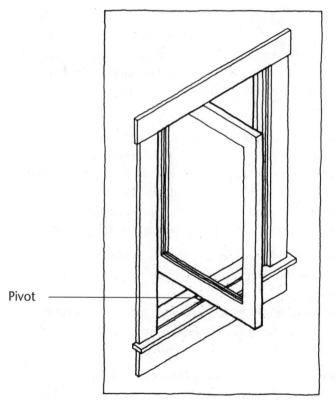

Pivot

DIAGRAM 48

114 WEIRD WINDOWS, LEADED GLASS

DIAGRAM 49

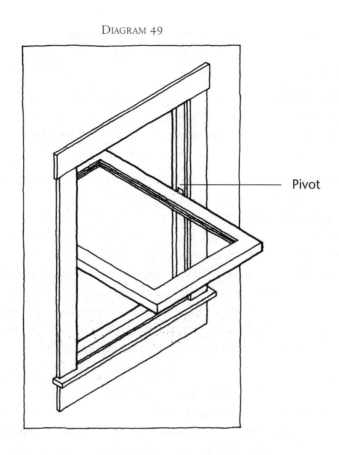

Pivot

LEADED WINDOWS

Many "leaded" windows are actually built with zinc cames (a came is the section of lead or zinc that has a channel in it for holding the glass). Lead was usually used with more elaborate stained-glass windows. Much of the residential leaded glass from the 1920s and 1930s, for instance, was fairly plain; just simple geometric design.

Originally, the space between the glass and the cames was filled with a cement-type material that, over time, deteriorates and falls out. The glass can loosen and air or water can seep in. Also, the joints can crack and the whole section can weaken. If your glass rattles when you tap on it or you can push in on the joints, you should consider some repairs.

What to do? Well, you can haul everything down to Mr. or Ms. Stained-Glass Artisan who, for a rate similar to a Mr. or Ms. Glazier, will solder the joints and tighten the glass. If a lot of work is involved, inquire about replacement costs.

Low budget? No budget? No problem. You can tighten the glass up easily enough. Take a putty knife and carefully dig out any loose material near the glass. Follow up with a brass brush to clean the came. Next, force a small amount of gray glazing compound into the came and smooth it out. The drawback to glazing compound is that it, too, will fall out if it isn't sealed. You can use an artist's brush and apply a narrow bead of exterior polyurethane or even an oil. Or you can use a dark gray latex caulk and carefully shoot it into the came using as small an opening in the tube as possible. Smooth the bead with a putty or glazing knife and wipe off the excess. You may prefer to use clear caulk.

Latex caulk is difficult to smooth out with a tool without smearing it on the glass, although this excess can be cleaned off with a razor blade. The caulk does a good job of sealing the glass and reinforcing all of the cames. If you ever have to replace a piece of glass, the caulking is a pain to remove and you will probably think malevolent thoughts about Mr. Window. Such is the price of offering an affordable fix for my readers.

If the joints are cracked, use a clear exterior polyurethane or other exotic caulk to secure the joint. No, this isn't as good as professionally resoldering, but it does help. If the joint is bad, even soldering can only improve it to a point, and if you cannot afford to replace the glass, you might as well caulk it and leave it at that. I am nothing if not practical. Caulking the cames on both sides of the glass will help strengthen weak cames even further.

Chapter Seven

A Final Word

I've only found one other book that addresses window repair and have listed it below. It was available at the local library and I have included my comments on it. *Old House Journal* is a good resource for historic homes and buildings, and periodically has articles on window maintenance. You'll prevent a lot of problems if you clarify the lead issues before doing your work. As one WISHA (our state version of OSHA) representative told me, "You can eat the stuff for lunch, I don't care. But if you ever have employees and expose them or other workers, your problems will increase exponentially." Her concern for my health was very touching.

- *Repairing Old and Historic Windows: A Manual for Architects and Homeowners*, by the New York Landmarks Conservancy (Washington, DC: The Preservation Press, National Trust for Historic Preservation, 1992).
  Mr. Window's one-minute review: More suited to older buildings than those on the West Coast. Includes steel windows, touches on repairs (one chapter, unlike the thoroughness and practicality of Mr. Window's book). Addresses energy conservation, storm windows, historic issues, window replacement.

- *Old House Journal*
  2 Main St.
  Gloucester, MA 01930
  Available at newsstands and libraries.

- *Old House Journal,* July-August 1992, "Getting Rid of Lead" by Marylee MacDonald.
  Call for reprints: 1-800-356-9313

- National Lead Abatement Center
  1-800-LEAD-FYI

- Contact your local health department or poison control center for additional information about lead and its hazards.

- The U.S. Government Printing Office (Washington, DC 20402) has various publications available from the U.S. Department of the Interior, National Park Service, Technical Preservation Services. They offer some background information and historic restoration guidelines (basically, save everything), but not much on how to do repairs.

DATE			